Over 40 women share inspiring st[...]es of [...]
determination, and persistent self-moti[...]ation to [...]

THE DECONSTRUCTING G.R.I.T. COLLECTION

GRIT
Tenacity

COMPILED BY
JENNIFER BARDOT

TENACITY - Deconstructing G.R.I.T. Collection
Over 40 women share inspiring stories of fearless courage, bold determination, and persistent self-motivation to achieve personal success.
MDC Press

Cover, Interior Design, and Project Management:
  Davis Creative Publishing, DavisCreativePublishing.com
Writing Coach and Editor: Maria Rodgers O'Rourke

Compilation by Jennifer Bardot

Publisher's Cataloging-in-Publication
(Provided by Cassidy Cataloguing Services, Inc.)
Names: Bardot, Jennifer, compiler.
Title: Tenacity : the deconstructing G.R.I.T. collection / compiled by Jennifer Bardot.
Other titles: Tenacity GRIT
Description: St. Louis, MO : MDC Press, [2023]
Identifiers: ISBN: 978-1-7371848-8-1 (paperback) | 978-1-7371848-9-8 (ebook) |
    LCCN: 2023920335
Subjects: LCSH: Determination (Personality trait)--Literary collections. | Determination
    (Personality trait)--Anecdotes. | Courage--Literary collections. | Courage--Anecdotes. |
    Persistence--Literary collections. | Persistence--Anecdotes. | Motivation (Psychology)--Lit-
    erary collections. | Motivation (Psychology)--Anecdotes. | Self-actualization (Psychology)
    in women--Literary collections. | Self-actualization (Psychology) in women--Anecdotes. |
    LCGFT: Anecdotes.
Classification: LCC: BF698.35.D48 T46 2023 | DDC: 158.1--dc23

I dedicate this book to my parents
as they have taught me, truly, to have G.R.I.T.
and how to be driven, dynamic
and to care for others.

— Jennifer Bardot —

Table of Contents

DRIVEN

Geared up and my engines are revving

First, Second, Third, Forth.

When I'm in fifth
and we are purring
my favorite sound exhausts roaring.

Feeling untouchable, Flying, Believing in myself.

Reaching top speeds of over 260mph.

A rush of adrenalin, a sonic boom, no brakes,
an unstoppable machine.

Fierce, fast, capable hands firmly on the wheel.

Where I dare to go, no speed limits exist, limitless, tenaciously fearless.

Burning rubber and not looking in the review mirror.

Jennifer McDonnell Bardot

Jennifer Bardot

Choose Your Speed Limits

If everything seems under control, you're just not going fast enough.
— Mario Andretti

There are two definitive moments in our lives: birth and death. Yet we have so much time in the "in between" to grow, evolve, thrive, and be tenacious. Time is never guaranteed, but we each have a choice about what we do with our time in the in between.

I like a good challenge, a rush of adrenaline, laughing a lot, creating positive change, advocating for others, creating hope, being with those that I love, and choosing to find joy in the little things. Good, bad, or ugly, the sun always rises day after day, and we have a choice to evolve and design how we live in the "in between."

It was 2003; I was nineteen and in Danton, Texas, with my father on a weekend trip with his friends from the St. Louis Corvette Club. I was excited for this trip as it was a twelve-hour drive with my dad traveling to the Texas Motor Speedway. Growing up with a love for cars, attending car shows, watching drag races, and going to several NASCAR races, the anticipation of being on the track was thrilling. When we arrived, we had an opportunity to walk the track and we saw that some of the professional racers were taking people out for rides at top speeds. With the encouragement of my dad's friends, and my desire to experience what it would be like to be a professional race car driver, I put on my racing suit and jumped in the passenger seat. G-forces pushed my back into the bucket seat, and adrenaline raced through my veins as the professional driver lapped the course. Those three laps passed quickly, and all I could do was trust the driver and look straight ahead. Terrified and filled with pure excitement experiencing these sound barrier–breaking speeds was unlike anything I had ever endured. As I looked through the netting over the window, the real world was a blur and all I could decipher was the circular track and tires burning rubber. By jumping into that passenger seat, I chose to evolve, live fearlessly, and have the courage to experience something new.

Shortly after regaining my balance, I was invited to drive on the motor speedway. With my dad's consent, I jumped into the driver's seat and drove my father around the track, not taking his car to the speeds I had experienced in the NASCAR, but faster than the highway speed limits. I saw the pride in my dad's eyes as I courageously drove the track at racing speeds! This experience is important to share because I was first in the passenger seat and then drove on the track, choosing to evolve and set my speed limit fearlessly. I live this way even today, by choosing to do things that scare me and allow me to evolve.

When I published my first anthology, *Owning Your G.R.I.T.*, I didn't have the courage to lead this project on my own. Yet the experience gave me the courage to get in the driver's seat and lead four more anthologies, independently supporting more than 207 women to publish their story. As I reflect on this work beginning with my choice to be tenacious, I've witnessed contributing authors jump into the driver's seat by publishing their own anthology, writing their own autobiography, starting a podcast, quitting their job to start their own business, or being reenergized from identifying their strength. My hope is that this ripple effect continues to create positive change in all who read these anthologies. If I can inspire others to be tenacious, choose to evolve, live fearlessly, and have the courage to create positive change, then I've succeeded. When we choose to grow, we indirectly impact others, and I am proud to say that because I jumped into publishing stories of G.R.I.T., I've personally developed more tenacity on my personal journey of supporting others to share their stories and whole-heartedly enjoyed seeing the growth of the contributing authors.

Have you ever believed something would happen, and after a few months or maybe years you see your manifestations become reality? This comes to pass by following three simple steps: 1) I can, 2) I will, and 3) I did. These steps will alter your mindset to sit in the driver's seat and help you accomplish great things, with no speed limits.

I've published five books from May 2021 through November 2023 because of a desire to infuse the world with G.R.I.T. after a two-year global sentence called the pandemic. Speeding through four successful published anthologies in fifteen months with a mission to amplify the voices of women has led me to launching *Tenacity*, which is my victory lap. Before the pandemic, had you ever been forced to stay at home? Not having control of your day, activities, and life changes a person. It gave us all time to reflect and identify our true passions but also brought about alarming rates of loneliness. As a species we thrive in community, and during this time of global isolation many were just trying to survive. This didn't leave much time for determining everyone's "in between." I choose to evolve by stepping into publishing hard stories to create hope by allevi-ating loneliness through finding similarities in our stories.

The more stories shared within this collection, the larger the impact and the more change was created.

"I Will." It was in April 2022. I chose to commit to building the *Deconstructing G.R.I.T. Collection*, a four-part series launching in August

2022, January 2023, and July 2023. This book is the "T" rounding out the collection on November 1, 2023. From the April 2021 launch of *Owning Your G.R.I.T.* to April 2022 was the one-year anniversary of kicking off my tenacious journey. These anthologies have grown to a collection featuring more than 207 women's stories. I've supported these women in stepping into publishing and witnessed changes experienced through sharing our stories. After fifteen months of authoring, publishing, recruiting, and curating ideas into reality, I've hit my goal and fulfilled my mission of supporting women's growth, making a global impact; but what's next for me is continuing to choose to evolve.

Leading these leaders, and navigating ongoing setbacks during the anthology project, have taught me numerous lessons. Remembering that my mission was greater than the setbacks helped me in choosing to keep moving forward. When the self-doubt would creep in, I would say, "Seldom does the safer play provide the results that you are seeking. Stay in route, commit, believe, and tackle anything that arises in your path." By harnessing my inner cheetah, I've successfully brought to the world the stories of women who have trusted me, and I have protected and supported them in writing their stories to feed and nourish the lives of others in our community.

"Use your fear, it can take you to the place where you store your courage."

-Amelia Earhart

Have you ever pushed yourself beyond your comfort zone, beyond the fear, because of a dream you envision so clearly you felt your entire soul giving everything you have to make that dream come true? When we have those pulls of attraction leading us to our utter purpose, we become fearless, unstoppable, limitless, and we can't even imagine anything derailing us from achieving our purpose. This is how I have felt since beginning of this journey to highlight women in our community who have shown the GRIT to inspire others. These stories have had a deep impact on readers who aren't able to talk about their struggles and alleviate their loneliness. This is a journey I've been called to: to heal our leaders from trauma and spark more to lead their life, achieve their goals, and provide our world with tools to navigate through hardships. It is guaranteed that a moment will come when life will toss us an obstacle but we have to keep driving. If we can train and become more prepared to navigate those potholes, we will be more capable of continuing our journey less tattered. That is my personal mission in amplifying the voices of all the women authors who contributed to the G.R.I.T. anthologies. As Joan of Arc said, "I am not afraid…I was born to do this."

Have you ever chosen to be fearless and turn a dream into reality? What is holding you back? Will this dream be something you are compelled to work toward daily, monthly, yearly, and dedicate yourself to wholeheartedly? Dream big, then dream bigger, and be courageous on your journey. Achieving it will require you to believe in yourself and in your mission, fearlessly and with dedication.

How are you going to begin to train yourself to have more mental tenacity?

Building mental strength is the fundamental best way to live your life. Just like going to the gym to build physical muscles, you must develop your mental strength with the tools and techniques. Optimal health requires social connections that are meaningful, and positive self-esteem.

Here are some tips to keep you in the driver's seat to tenaciously follow your dreams:

1. Positive thinking and limitless mindset

2. Control emotions, push through fear

3. Manifest your objective

4. Just go; getting started is key

Jennifer Bardot, MA, MS, is a publisher of the *Deconstructing GRIT Collection* (*Growth, Resilience, Intention & Tenacity*) and *Owning Your G.R.I.T.*—all international bestselling anthologies. She was featured on ABC, CBS, Fox, and NBC, on VoiceAmerica, the cover of *St. Louis Small Business Monthly* as 2021's 100 St. Louisans You Should Know to Succeed in Business, and was awarded the President's Circle by Enterprise Bank & Trust. Founder of the GRIT Community—a free women's leadership group—Jennifer holds a bachelor's degree and dual master's degrees, certificates in the Dare to Lead Training by Brené Brown, Women in Leadership Class of '72, and Leadership St. Louis by Focus St. Louis. She serves Lindenwood University on the MentorUp committee, Washington University as a financial expert on behalf of the Skandalaris Center, and Fontbonne University on the Employer & Community Partnership Council. Jennifer is passionate about supporting business owners and female leaders, and is a dedicated mother, community connector, and outdoor adrenaline adventurer.

Cathy Davis

The Way of the Imagineer

Approximately twenty years ago, near the end of my corporate career with a global financial services company, I was on a business flight to "somewhere," seated next to a Disney Imagineer. I was enthralled with the concept of working for Disney, let alone the title of: "Imagineer!" Our conversation that day was more than likely the "seed" that later motivated me to take a leap of faith, start my own business, and leave the corporate world behind.

What I remember most about our conversation on the flight is that much like a four-year-old, I asked a thousand questions about his job. As he explained it, most of the time his job required him to "imagine the possibilities" and ask "What if...?" or "How about...?" or "Why not...?" questions. His saw his role as one where he constantly pushed himself to think outside the box and expand the perceived boundaries of both his direct reports as well as his managers. If someone had a grand idea, he did everything in his power to turn it into reality.

He shared that all ideas were welcome and there was usually always a way to make those ideas happen. He talked about how he was also the "Chief Re-Framer," meaning whenever a team member or manager would respond with "Can't do it!" or "We've never done that before!" it signaled his own determination and tenacity to prove them wrong and make sure his vision came to fruition. Most often, he'd respond with, "Let's find a way!"

Not too long after that plane ride, I was laid off. The marketing services department I had worked in for more than twelve years was shut down in December of 2003. I decided to become a self-employed branding consultant. The ensuing years have had many ups and downs, but as I gained determination and tenacity, the "ups" became more frequent, and the "downs" became fewer.

As the twentieth anniversary of my independent employment approaches, I reflect on my own journey through the past two decades of entrepreneurship, and I notice definite patterns of growth. I can see where I would move in and out of trusting myself—almost as if I was wandering through trying to run a business. I would frequently find myself falling into F.A.D.—Fear, Anxiety, and Doubt. I was navigating territory I'd never been in, often calling myself the "Reluctant Entrepreneur!"

Early on, when life handed me rotten apples, I now see how my response was typically more from the "victim" mode. With more experience and years behind me—including at least three business coaches—I eventually learned I could reframe the negative F.A.D. of Fear, Anxiety, and Doubt and turn it around into the more positive message of Fearless, Audacious, and Determined! Then, what I saw as rotten apples were merely life lessons helping me grow more into the role of an Imagineer.

My transition into an Imagineer evolved out of three phases:

Determined to Do it By Myself!

The very first lesson I needed to learn was that I did not need to try and do it all by myself. A haphazard childhood taught me to be overly self-responsible. Growing up, I did a lot for myself and unfortunately learned to not rely upon others for assistance. When life became stressful or I felt overwhelmed, I hesitated to ask for help. Hesitation is the opposite of tenacity and was my unconscious way of putting the brakes on growing my business. After all, why would I dare venture deeper into the unknown? My comfort zone was in holding on to what I knew. The unfortunate side of hesitation is remaining too independent and not knowing when to ask for help. I focused on the problems, and therefore the problems increased—not yet realizing that if I had focused on the solutions, the solutions would have increased!

During that first decade of working for myself, the Universe tossed several proverbial "bricks upside the head" my way, which I dutifully navigated all by myself—which was all that I knew to do:

- My mother fell, broke her hip, and we moved her from an apartment to a nursing home; I was the designated sibling (aka: only volunteer) to manage the transition.
- My husband was downsized and also began working for himself; our steady stream of income became nonexistent.
- My mother passed away. Again, I was the designated sibling to handle the details and take care of cleaning out her room, her storage, and eight-plus decades of papers and memories.
- My husband was diagnosed with cancer three months after my mother passed (eighteen months of treatment and a cancer survivor today). Again, I was the one left in charge, juggling the workload as well as the patient at-home recovery.

Learned to Ask for Help!

I found myself drained, depressed, and depleted. Out of desperation, it was time to stretch my Trust Box and imagine the possibilities. The second lesson I needed to learn was to ask for help. Eventually I realized there really are people out there who are willing to help. My tenacity kicked in, and I started setting better boundaries—I took a chance and reached out to both of my siblings, asking for help with my mother. Although both lived out of state and could not physically be here in person, each gave in ways that they could, and I grew to trust each a bit more.

My business was hurting because my attention was stretched elsewhere. I finally hired my first business coach in 2016, joined a mastermind, and focused on growing my business. I found a business coach in New York who had a similar mindset and values—and was running her own successful business. Once again, I was learning to stretch my Trust Box and be willing to rely upon the experience of more seasoned business owners. Over the years, I have worked with a handful of business coaches, learning invaluable lessons and best practices from each.

Most importantly, I was not willing to quit. Historically, the closer I would get to success, whether at school, a job, or in a relationship, I'd "jump ship" and move on to something new. When it came to the success of my business, I believed the answers were just around the corner, and I needed to keep looking, asking, and believing. The more I believed I could be successful, the more success showed up. I was becoming boldly tenacious in looking for solutions and new ways to expand my business.

Began to Imagine!

In my second decade of entrepreneurship, as I was determined to make my business profitable and successful, my confidence grew, and so did the trust in myself. I learned to trust the little girl who had earlier learned to parent herself. I learned to reparent her as needed, offering the support and encouragement she didn't get when growing up. My tenacity grew alongside my confidence, and I eagerly stepped into the role of the Imagineer. I found my comfort zone and learned my life could be whatever I imagined.

The most dramatic change in my business came in 2020 when I began taking classes in NLP (Neuro-Linguistic Programming). A long-time bucket list item for me, the several-month training emphasized a positive mindset, strategies for reframing negative situations, and most of all provided a sense of self-confidence needed to grow one's business. I learned to release the earlier-proclaimed title of "Reluctant Entrepreneur" and wholeheartedly began to claim "Imagineer!"

An Imagineer in today's world:

- Dreams BIG.
- Allows their imagination to soar.
- Believes everything is possible.
- Sets intentions and makes things happen.
- Creates a vision and takes action in that direction.
- Reframes negative energy into a positive vision.
- Adds an element of play to brighten each day.
- Paints their world with rainbow colors.
- Follows their heart and listens to their intuition.
- Believes in magic and shares it!

Today's Imagineers tenaciously turn ideas and dreams into reality!

I still have that business card from the Disney Imagineer. Its presence in a desk drawer is a frequent reminder to believe in myself, surround myself with other Imagineers, and to be tenacious in making magic happen. I'm still learning, and just as I figure one thing out, a new lesson pops up for me to navigate. One thing I know for sure—I alone am responsible for the magic in my life (or lack thereof).

I invite you to join me as an Imagineer of Life, and let's see what the next decade will bring!

Books are in Cathy's DNA and have always played a big role in her life. Cathy Davis believes we all have a story to tell, and it is through sharing our stories that we can make a difference in the lives of others. Wisdom not shared is wisdom lost forever.

Cathy founded Davis Creative, LLC in January of 2004 after spending the bulk of her corporate career as Designer and Creative Director for a global wealth management institution. Publishing their first book for a client in 2005, Davis Creative Publishing Partners is now a sought-after publishing industry leader, working with speakers, leaders, healers, coaches, and consultants to publish books that share their wisdom, inspire more people, and make a difference in the world.

With clients around the corner and around the world, Cathy and her team have helped more than a thousand authors become published, with close to five hundred being International Bestselling authors.

Ashley Nelson

You Do You

I've always been drawn to the uphill battle. Something about the challenge, but most notably the thrill of accomplishment. I like to think I'm a version of an adrenaline junkie—just not the jumping out of planes or bungee-jumping type. I get my kicks out of breaking barriers, encouraging the underdogs, and watching the disbelief on the doubters' face when the sweet victory of accomplishment is achieved. Perhaps my most favorite is when someone says you can't, you shouldn't, or you're going to have to choose; this is when I hear a battle cry in my head and the "hold my beer" mentality kicks in. This is my personal anthem for tenacity: a sense of pride that showcases who you are versus trying to suppress your true self to match what others think you should be. Tenacity allows this authentic unveiling to happen.

Where did this mindset come from? It's a culmination of life experiences.

My mom would certainly like to know the answer to this question. My tenacity started when I was three years old. I remember overhearing a conversation that sounded to my young self like an argument between my mom and grandmother. I listened from the back bedroom where I was supposed to be taking a nap. Instead, I whipped around the corner in my two-piece rainbow 80s outfit with my hand on my hip and proclaimed,

"Don't be talking to my mama like that!" The conversation stopped, their heads slowly turned, and they stared at me, stunned. I stared right back without blinking, hand on hip still, of course. We stayed in this stalemate for a few more seconds before I went back to the bedroom and settled in for my nap.

I can distinctly remember feeling a rush of emotion, which was quite confusing at my young age. That was the moment I learned the value of being fierce. Clearly, the tact and curtness of the message left a bit to be desired, but for a three-year-old, it was authentic and clear. There is power in using your voice, standing up for what you believe in, and defending those who you adore, at any age.

Here is the thing about being fierce; it is a perfect blend of grit, persistence, and nourishing a tenacious spirit. As a woman, it can be interpreted as manipulating, arrogant, or aggressive. I see it as boldness, advocacy, and confidence, and I became impassioned with shattering this stigma.

Call it fate or manifestation of circumstance, but I somehow always managed to find myself knocking on the door of traditionally male-dominated opportunities.

In college, I worked at a local eatery and was ready to be promoted to cashier from food runner and floor sweeper. While these are all very important jobs, they weren't fulfilling my career desires. A friend who worked for a car dealership told me they were hiring a car salesperson. He asked if I knew of anyone. I said, "You are staring right at her." He laughed, and I looked him in the eye and said, "No, I am serious."

Walking into the showroom on my first day, I passed by a group of middle-aged men staring in disbelief that the new salesperson could very well be their daughter, which made for an interesting introduction. My response, "Gentlemen, let's do this."

I knew I was going to have a particularly large learning curve and uphill resistance overcoming gender bias of a traditional car sales "man," but I was ready.

I took sweet joy in the skepticism on a particular customer's face when he asked me to go get the "real" salesperson when I met him on the asphalt of the lot—the new-car section. It was an unusually hot day, and his patience level was at an all-time low. He told me he needed someone who "actually" knew something about cars to come out. I firmly grasped onto my tenacity and confidently told him I was that person. I calmly explained the nearly 300 horsepower, 260 torque, V6 engine that was available in both manual and automatic transmission, and that whatever specifications he desired would certainly be the perfect combination of both performance and luxury.

The slight curl of his wife's mouth into a half smile when she silently locked eyes with me for a brief moment during the explanation said everything.

Can you look back in your life and see how many experiences or opportunities you would have missed if you were waiting for the invitation? When I look back in history to those celebrated leaders, the standouts were not the ones who were asking for permission. They were the ones who were fueled with passion, drive, desire, and the bravery to be bold. Their tenacious spirit achieved a legacy of brilliance and inspiration.

At the age of thirty, I became the top human resources executive at a manufacturing company and was responsible for thousands of lives with the opportunity to make a marked difference. I was also pregnant with our first child and due any day. Many women feel they must make a choice—to be a present parent or have a career. If you want to choose to do either or both, that is great. But the key is having a choice to begin with and to not be judged for the choice that you make.

This became my mission—if not only for me, then for the baby about to be born into a world where I wanted there to be an option for "and" not just "or." For me and many parents, we live our lives for the legacy, for the impressionable experiences, and the "remember when" moments our children will reminisce about in our honor.

I am glad I chose "and." While my husband was supportive and my company was supportive, were there doubters? Sure. My age, coupled with being a new mom in an executive role, made some say I was too young to handle it all. My response: this was an opportunity for a new perspective. Some said: "How will you have enough time?" My answer: "Have you witnessed the mastery of a multitasking mom before?" Some said: "How will you be present to them at home when there is much work to do?" My answer: "Boundaries." As a bonus, I learned some incredible time-management skills while simultaneously managing a breast milk–pumping and business meeting schedule.

It was at that moment that I decided that the naysayers do not get to write my rules. You are the author of your own story. You write your own chapters. You label your own pages. And the most rewarding part has been the numerous people who have come to me and said, "I saw you do it, so it gave me hope that I could do it too." Inspiration is powerful. We are not only living for ourselves, but we are honoring those who came before us and paving the path for those who will come after us.

So where does your journey to accomplishment through tenacity start?

Does this new opportunity make you nervous? Does it make you uncomfortable? Does it cause that voice in your head to say, "Maybe I can't" or "I shouldn't"? The answer: Lean in and do more of those things. Find your passion and fuel it. When you become comfortable falling into failure, you'll realize that every experience, although sometimes not fully the desired outcome, brings learning, and builds both confidence and the new cornerstone that supports who you are. Building a tenacious mindset bolsters an attitude of simply never giving up.

Cheers to the risk takers, the authentic thought thinkers, and the ones who stand alone in the crowd because they know it's the right choice and not the popular one. To the ones who will say "yes" even though "no" is easier and more comfortable. To the ones who intentionally put themselves in uncomfortable situations because the excitement for growth outweighs the burden of fear.

Our lives are an incubator of experiences, and we must learn to accept ourselves for our strengths, laugh at our faults, and garner inspiration from defeat. Everyone has a story. Even simple moments can have lifelong impacts. One of the most rewarding feelings is to be your complete and authentic self—not who others think you should be or want you to be, but exactly who you are.

So, you do *you*. With a hand on your hip, of course.

Ashley Nelson is an innovative, results-driven leader. As the Chief Human Resources Officer of a refrigeration manufacturer based in the Midwest, she supports domestic and global business initiatives by executing people-focused programs and practices to achieve the organization's goals. Ashley is dedicated to modernizing and transforming the human resources function, which is fueled by her passion for continuous improvement and influencing organizational change. Ashley has more than fifteen years of HR experience in the manufacturing industry.

She holds a bachelor's degree from Missouri State University, a master's degree from Lindenwood University, and is PHR and SHRM-CP certified. She serves on the executive board for the O'Fallon Chamber of Commerce and Industries.

Ashley lives in Kirkwood, Missouri, with her husband and two children. She and her husband own a real estate investment business named after their two sons, Henry and Harrison. When not at the baseball fields or soccer park, they enjoy traveling the globe experiencing new cultures and food.

Farica Chang

Infinite Mindset

It started as a trickle.

Eight months, two weeks, and one day pregnant with my first child. When I imagined my water breaking, I envisioned it like a balloon popping, a gush of fluid as a clear indicator my baby was ready to make her grand entrance into the world. What I got instead was a tiny nudge—nothing that made me realize in all my unpreparedness that the time was now.

I brushed aside any notion of being in labor and prepared to go into the office as if it were any other day. I didn't mention anything to my husband, Chris. What was the point? As managing partner at rapidly growing technology consulting firms, Anderson Technologies and Anderson Archival, I had too many other important issues on my mind to pay attention to something so insignificant. I was racing to ensure my team had everything they needed to keep running when the baby arrived. I anticipated being out of the office for two weeks at most. This is how little I knew about newborns.

Instead, the months that followed took me to the brink of pain and exhaustion while simultaneously manifesting love and strength beyond what I thought possible. As many already know, becoming a parent transforms you, and when that path starts with uncertainty, it forces you to recognize new truths. The motivators that compel tenacity kick into over-drive when a new life depends on how well you react to adversity.

When I finally got around to calling the doctor's office to let them know about my trickle, they suggested going to the Labor and Delivery wing just in case. Chris and I took our time. I was sure I should be feeling more pain. My pregnancy had been blissfully absent of morning sickness, cramps, or much discomfort. We joked they would turn us around immediately with a false alarm. Instead, the nurse took one look at me and said, "Oh, your water's broken all right," and that's when the wheels started spinning. Soon, the heart rate monitor around my belly began to alarm, and suddenly my doctor calmly informed us I needed an emergency C-section. Less than thirty minutes after arriving at the hospital, I was in shock, awake on an operating room table, and no longer able to feel the lower half of my body. With my husband by my side, our daughter, Kaia, was pulled into the world with a loud, healthy cry.

While they stitched me back up, Chris cut her umbilical cord, and the nurses measured and bundled her. They gave her to me for sweet skin-on-skin time while the operating room team completed their tasks. The three of us wrapped each other in a loving embrace thinking the worst was over. Little did we know it was just beginning.

As soon as we returned to our room, the nurses began taking blood samples from Kaia. They flagged her blood sugar as dangerously low and wheeled her off to the NICU before we could get a word in. At the same time, they took my blood pressure and said it was dangerously high, something that can happen postpartum, though I'm sure having my daughter immediately transferred away had some effect as well.

They hooked me to a drip of magnesium sulfate fed directly through my IV. It felt like fire coursing through my veins. The solution's intended purpose to lower my blood pressure and prevent seizures felt inconsequential. The list of additional side effects is long and terrible. Kaia also had an IV in her tiny arm for a steady intake of sugar solution. Numbers trapped both of us. Hers came in the form of blood pricks to her heels every three hours—measuring her sugar—each time determining her fate for the ensuing three hours. This included inserting a nasogastric tube down her throat for feeding to maintain her levels. Mine came from the blood pressure cuff, setting the bar for when I could be released from the hospital. We went on like this for days. My concern for Kaia, searing pain, and fatigue fed my heightened numbers.

Subconsciously, I knew the hospital team sought our well-being. At the time, however, I felt captive—unable to free myself and my daughter to start our new family life at home without passing seemingly arbitrary tests. The treatments attempting to lower my blood pressure affected me worse than the issue, and every time Chris wheelchaired me to see Kaia hooked up to so many monitors with the tube taped up her nose and her poor feet pricked to oblivion, I cried tears of frustration and exhaustion. Things seemed hopeless.

As the firstborn daughter of parents who immigrated to Missouri from Hong Kong with nothing, I have spent my whole life pushing myself to work hard and improve upon yesterday. Before Kaia, my job was my life. I loved it and still do. Starting as a part-time contractor in 2008 and becoming managing partner in 2018, I regularly devoted seventy to eighty hours per week to achieving goals and trying to create the best possible environment for my team. In the weeks leading up to Kaia's birth, I continued—even working all night until three a.m. to solve an unexpected problem with a client's cloud email migration. There is always an answer, even if you sometimes must press your limits to find it.

Our company is guided by our core values. We live them every day, and hire, fire, and reward our team based on them. As the days began to turn to weeks in the hospital, I reflected on one of my favorites, Infinite Mindset, defined as:

We believe in the limitless supply of ideas. Each of us possess the innate ability to be immeasurably great. We believe there is a solution for every challenge no matter how daunting it may first seem. With a sense of infinity and love for all, our lives serve as shining lights to defeat frustration and doubt.

This is what ultimately freed and prepared me for the challenges we faced in the ensuing months. After cycles upon three-hour cycles of measurements, I found a way to release the trapped hopelessness coursing through me since the day Kaia arrived. Giving in to the situation was not an option. I knew I needed to push past the negativity plaguing me since the whirlwind of her unexpected arrival and focus on the good. Once I did, a weight lifted, replaced by the calm certainty I needed to pass the tests that confined me to the hospital bed.

The months following our release were far from easy. After weeks of knowing life a certain way in the NICU, adjusting to the daily surprises that come with a special newborn became another rollercoaster of emotions. It was the ultimate test of tenacity for me—balancing feeding Kaia, pumping milk, caring for her, cleaning up a seemingly endless stream of baby vomit, taking her to numerous appointments, and continuing to work, to put on a strong, brave leader face despite everything. Even at the hospital hours after her birth, I kept working. Although I had recently welcomed a baby under extraordinary circumstances, it never crossed my mind to step back from my critical duties as a managing partner. Leading a small business means wearing many hats. The success of our rapidly expanding firm depended on me, and I continually feel an enormous responsibility for my colleagues and our clients. I was determined not to let my daughter or my business down. I stretched myself to my limits, giving Kaia all the loving care I could. While she slept, I worked to lead my firm to its most successful year ever. The first nine months of Kaia's life are a blur of exhaustion wrapped in layers of dedication to my daughter, my family, my team, and my company.

What makes us tenacious? What gives us the willpower to get through difficult times? When we are tested, we become the ultimate examples of mind over matter, of grit powered by love to see the opportunities within seemingly impossible situations. Love is the driver of all that is pure. It fuels our ability to overcome and persist. In the times I feel "less than" or like an utter failure at balancing motherhood and business leadership, I reflect on the love that pushed me to where I am today. I remind myself of our innate ability to be infinite, to look past the uncertainty and see the light. I share my vulnerabilities, and instead of drowning I'm buoyed by the support of my husband, my family, and my team. They rally to fill in the gaps I can't manage as I juggle my time and my capacity.

Now, over a year since Kaia's birth, she is a perfect, healthy child intent on pushing her boundaries like any other toddler. As she explores this gift of a world, she reflects infinite mindset and tenacity in their purest forms; she's my reminder for why we do what we do to prevail over hardship. For me, no other life lesson has been harder fought or harder won.

Farica Chang is a Principal at Anderson Technologies and Anderson Archival, IT consulting and digital preservation companies that excel in providing technology solutions designed to remove limitations.

Since joining the company immediately after graduating with honors from UCLA, Farica finds herself continually fascinated by the ever-changing world of technology and the challenge of crafting processes to deliver services of all shapes and sizes in ways that exceed expectations.

Her dedication to her team has created a culture of care, loyalty, optimism, and initiative that radiates from the core of everything the company offers—whether that is outstanding IT support, project consulting, or historical media preservation and presentation. Farica leads a growing group of bright individuals who appreciate being able to collaborate without ego to find creative solutions.

When not working, Farica is learning how to balance life as a managing partner with motherhood after she and her husband welcomed a daughter in 2022.

Jennifer Church

I WIN

I will win. Each and every single time, I will win. It may not be an immediate win, but I will absolutely and definitely win what I want. It's not over until I win. That is the mindset of a tenacious person. That is me.

Now keep in mind that winning does not always come with a blue ribbon or a gold medal. It doesn't always mean you crossed the finish line first, got the highest score, or achieved your goal in record time. Sometimes even taking the loss is the win! Winning comes in many shapes and sizes. Defining it depends on how you look at it.

I like to look at winning by seeing forward progress and doing better than the time before or truly learning a lesson. It is about achieving more than you have in the past. Winning is about not giving up, ever. No matter what the obstacles are, how great the fear is, or how difficult it is. A tenacious person recognizes there is no amount of failure that can stop you. If it doesn't work out, you should regroup and try again with an improved method. Never stop trying.

I remember a day when I was feeling defeated like I'd never get out from under the dilemma I was facing. So I took a good look in the mirror and asked the teary-eyed reflection staring back at me, "How many times are you willing to recover from failure, Jennifer?" "Every. Single. Time," I mouthed back to myself. Even though I continued to stand there and cry my eyes out, I knew that was the end of the tears, the last bit of pity and sorrow I would allow for this situation. I had to dig deep and change my mindset.

Nothing happens to me; all of it happens for me. For me to learn from it, to grow from it. We all know we cannot change the past, we can only learn from it. We have to understand that struggle and pain is there for a reason. You cannot experience strength without struggle. You cannot advance without adversity. Out of difficulty comes destiny. We must all go through something in order to get to something. Look at the past and assign a positive meaning to it instead of being the victim. Take any challenging situation and use it as a catalyst to set yourself up and propel yourself into a bright future.

Learning the skill of tenacity and applying it in your everyday life sets you apart. Knowing that failure doesn't define you will set you apart. Some of us accept failure, and the rest of us are hungry for the taste of success, accomplishment, and the pride that comes with it. I have witnessed a common denominator for every successful person I have come across in my life. Can you guess what it is? Yes, tenacity.

Tenacity isn't a trait; it's a mindset. It comes from training your mind to win. Tenacity is the determination of a person who will not give up when the possibility of succeeding becomes difficult or seems impossible to overcome. Go hard. Focus on the goal. Reach your goal and then diversify it into more, expand on it and win.

I can still see my eighth-grade class motto strung up in the front of the classroom on a giant banner above the chalkboard—"A winner never quits and a quitter never wins." Every morning, Mrs. Rygelski would start our day with three things. They were rituals. Our morning prayer, the Pledge of Allegiance, and reciting our motto. A winner never quits and a quitter never wins. That was in 1985, and I still think about that all the time. She was instilling tenacity in all of us. Thank you, Mrs. Rygelski, for teaching me the mindset of being tenacious. I have kept that lesson with me for my lifetime.

I don't listen much to what people say. I watch what they do. I pay attention to their actions and their mannerisms, and, inevitably, it will show you their character. I have learned saying something is the easiest part. Doing it is the hardest part. Showing up, time after time, and doing whatever it takes to make it work, to exceed the goal, to win. Again, it is tenacity.

I run across this all the time. The people in my life are very tenacious. This is a funny example, but it sticks with me. I remember a conversation with my sister, Jamie. I walked into her office and saw her watching her computer screen intently. I said, "Hey Jamie, what are you working on?" She replied with a snicker, "I'm playing 'I win.'" I laughed and said, "You're playing what?" She said "Oh, it's eBay, but I call it 'I win' because I will not give up until the last second of the bidding and I always win what I want." Of course, my sister won the bid and the item was hers. She said "See, I win!" She is a fantastic role model for me in so many ways, including being tenacious. That conversation was probably fifteen years ago, and I still call eBay "I win." Winning is a mindset; it is a goal. So whether you are buying something on eBay or achieving a goal to succeed at your dreams, it all comes down to staying the course regardless of how choppy the seas are.

I think the greatest example of tenacity I have ever witnessed is from Paul, my love. Our story is pretty neat. We grew up together, kind of. I met him the summer when I was twelve years old, almost thirteen. We had recently moved to a new neighborhood, and I met him at the local swimming pool. He and his friends were playing catch with their squishy ball adjacent to me and my friends. Paul was a very good baseball player, but somehow he missed the ball every single time his friends threw it to him that day. Mysteriously the ball always landed right in front of me. I must have handed him the ball back at least forty times. He was the cutest boy at the pool, and I remember it like it was yesterday. Well, long story short, he was the first boy I ever kissed. In true young-love fashion, our summer romance (if you can call a couple of kisses and holding hands a romance) ended when school started. He was a year older than I was and he went to a different school. So we rode our bikes off in different directions, and that was that.

We went our separate ways for many years—close to thirty-eight years, as a matter of fact. When we reconnected, we both had thirty-eight years of both good and bad experiences under our belts.

I was pretty much in shambles when we reconnected. I was somewhat of a train wreck—not financially or mentally, but an emotional train wreck. I had been through a terrible breakup a year prior and really couldn't wrap my head around all that had happened. It took a long time to reorganize this in my brain and find the perspective that nothing happened to me; all of it happened for me. For me to learn from this, to grow from it. It happened for me to understand that wasn't the place I was supposed to be anymore. Bigger and better things were to come.

Paul is tenacious. He was determined to make it through anything with me. He was patient and, most of all, kind. He is a gentle and sweet soul. He is exactly the person I needed in my life, although I did not want to admit that at the time. Paul and I could talk about anything, and we did; we do. We laughed and cried. We agreed, we argued, we even broke up a time or two. Yet he stayed the course, no matter what. He was always there with a sweet smile, an encouraging word, or the world's greatest hug. He could not have been more determined to be there for me no matter what. He didn't try to sell me or convince me of anything; he showed me over and over again that he was a great man. His actions spoke so much louder than his words. He proved that I could trust him and depend on him. Paul was a fantastic example of unconditional love. He made me feel safe, like I had never felt before.

I know it was not easy to love me then, but he did. He caught anything and everything I threw in his direction, good or bad. It is because of Paul and the love and determination he has shown to me that we are together today. He never gave up on me, and he never gave up on us.

Paul is a one-in-a-million kind of man, and I am so very fortunate that he is in my life, forever. So again, I win! Each and every single time. As I said, it may not be an immediate win, but I will absolutely and definitely win. That is the mindset of a tenacious person. "I Win" is a learned skill that requires tenacity. And often a bit of patience. Try it!

Jennifer Church currently resides in St. Louis, Missouri, where she was born and raised. Morgan, her daughter, is her greatest love. She is in the role of Strategic Account Manager with United Rentals, a Fortune 500 company that she has called home for more than twenty years. She is a Past President of The American Sub-Contractors Association Midwest Council. She currently sits on the national board of directors for the American Sub-Contractors and is an internationally multi-bestselling author. Her favorite hobbies include being with family and friends, golfing, boating, and art.

Gina Sweet

Beautifully Broken

During my sophomore year, I transferred to a new high school. This change would forever impact my life in a tenacious manner, and to this day it ripples waves of blessings in my life. My heart was broken by a boy named John Sweet, who took a love letter I wrote him, made copies of it, and passed it around my old high school. I had been signing "Gina Sweet" in my journals and notebooks since we met in seventh grade. I loved that boy and had poured my heart into the letter. Life was miserable. My step-dad took me to register at the new school and picked out my new classes for me. "JROTC?" I asked. "It's military training," he said. I felt helpless as I shrugged in compliance.

The U.S. Army Junior Reserve Officer Training Corps (JROTC) is a military-themed elective course program that teaches high school students the value of citizenship, leadership, and personal responsibility to their community through Army core values, physical training, and self-discipline. I desperately needed friends in a new school, and in JROTC I immediately found community. I had been given a clean slate; no one had to know my embarrassment from my old high school. Thank the good Lord we didn't have social media then! I tucked away the pain of John Sweet and took a firm grip on who I wanted to be. The first time I tried on my ROTC uniform was the first time I felt comfortable in my own skin. My eyes were opened to a potential future in the military and away from the hell I was living at home. Before I go any further, I must say that the next part of my story is very hard to share. It's taken many years and God's amazing grace to come to terms with my past. I now live in the light of the cross of Jesus Christ and try to live life all for his glory. I encourage you to tenaciously lean into the pains in life and grow through what you go through.

My parents moved to Miami, Florida, from Bogota, Colombia, when I was four years old. When I was eight, my father, in an alcohol-induced rage, kicked us out of our home. He moved back to Colombia when I was nine and passed away when I was thirteen. His departure left my mother and I illegal immigrants. I spent a lot of time home alone or in the back seat of my mother's car. This is when I began to feel my mother's neglect. She eventually applied for naturalization (becoming a U.S. citizen) and settled into sales. She became one of Mary Kay's top saleswomen and earned several pink Cadillacs. I admired my mother. I wanted her love, validation, and approval more than anything.

JROTC extracurricular activities included the after-school drill team program. One of the aspects of drill team was drill and ceremony, which is how a commander moves a unit of soldiers from one place to another in an orderly and precise manner with and without weapons. I competed at the national level as Regulation Drill Team Commander. In our senior year, our female drill team brought home the first place national title. This was the last of many competitions and the first one my mother ever attended. Before leaving for Nationals, I received a letter from the only university I had applied to. The letter stated that unfortunately I would have to apply as an international student since I wasn't a U.S. citizen. I couldn't afford this financially. I had to come to terms with the fact that after graduation I would lose my student visa here in the U.S. and, with no ability to legally work, would face deportation if at any time I were to need to prove my identity. My dreams of joining the military were crushed, along with any trust I had in my mother. There was no way I could go back to Colombia. To whom would I go? I felt invisible and lost at sea!

My lifelong friend Tony would prove to be the answer. He lived on the same floor of my apartment building a few doors down. Our moms met on June 15th, when Tony and I were each celebrating our fifth birthdays! As birthday buddies we shared more than our birthdate; we shared our childhood, and many of life's ups and downs. Tony was the brother I never had. When I told Tony about my situation, he offered to marry me and help me become a U.S. citizen, no strings attached. We graduated high school and got married a month later. He moved to Key West, and I stayed in Miami.

Life at home with my mother was tormenting. My stepdad had walked out when my baby sister was six months, and she was now four years of age. I tried running away several times as a teen but always came back for my baby sister. My mother would find me and remind me of how much my sister needed me. This time I couldn't take it anymore. As my mother raised her hand to slap me, I stopped her and told her I was done. I packed my things and left.

The whole immigration process was incredibly daunting. One intense interview sent me into weeks of depression where I dealt with suicidal ideations for months. The naturalization process forced Tony and I to move in with his family to validate our marriage. I was in over my head; this stuff was serious, and now I faced deportation or jail time if this wasn't a real marriage. Tony's family took me in. I love them! I grew so much during this time. I worked hard and learned to support myself. I dreamed of the day when I could leave Florida and join the military. I would close my eyes and see myself in my uniform. I was so ready to throw in the towel, and then one day I opened a letter with my green card in it.

It was May 2001, and Nelly Furtado's "I'm like a Bird" was playing in the taxicab that picked me up to take me to MEPS (Military Entrance Processing Station). From there I would be taken to the airport to travel to Fort Leonard Wood, Missouri, for basic training. The song lyrics "I'm like a bird, I'll only fly away. I don't know where my home is" brought tears to my eyes as I realized I was free. This was no longer my cage/home. I was doing what I had so tenaciously dared to dream. My life was finally in my hands.

During the last weeks of my military training, 9/11 took place. At my first duty station in Fort Riley, Kansas, they asked for volunteers to go to Kuwait in support of Operation Enduring Freedom. I remembered all the times I had considered taking my life and thought this would be a good way to amend those thoughts and, if so, die with honor. I volunteered and began training for deployment. During this time, I'd become romantically involved with a soldier who had become physically abusive; for anonymity we will call him G. I didn't report it, thinking I would escape him once I left for Kuwait. One day while at work I met a soldier with the last name Sweet. The pain I had tucked away from John Sweet's jerk move back in high school came flooding back. I asked him, "Do you have a relative named John by any chance?" He said no, of course. We became friends that day. One night he rescued me from an altercation with G. I didn't own a car, and Jason Sweet came in clutch that night with a smile that could win you over in a heartbeat. The next day he told me I would be his wife someday. I thought he was out of his mind. Two weeks into our deployment, I found out I was pregnant with G's baby. I called G, and he didn't want to speak to me. End of conversation. Next, I called my mother. She made it clear: get rid of it or forget you have a mother.

I was more than three months pregnant when I left Kuwait and traveled to Miami, where my mother picked me up from the airport and took me to the abortion clinic. I had tried to gain her acceptance and support for months to no avail. Afterwards I went back to Kuwait to finish my deployment. Sweet was sent to pick me up and take me back to the desert. There he was again, with his smile. Sweet saw me at my worst. He was the first person in my young life to show me unconditional love. Looking back, I can connect the dots of God's faithfulness in every heartbreak: being abandoned, disowned, unhoused, abused, ridiculed, and rejected, including by John Sweet. Daily I am reminded of his faithfulness.

I became Gina Sweet after all! Who would have thought that such a devastating heartbreak would lead to the most amazing breakthroughs in my life? Not me! Jason and I have been married now for twenty years. We have the most beautiful life together. We have five G.R.I.T.-y kids and live our lives with an ever-growing gratitude, resilience, intention, and tenacity. We have come to understand that grit is born in the valleys of life. Then we must look up to where our help comes from, plant our knees firmly in the ground, and remember:

"And we know that God causes everything to work together for the good of

Those who love God and are called according to his purpose for them."

Romans 8:28 (NLT)

My friend, I pray you are encouraged and filled with strength. May you glean courage and hope from this little message and remember that Our Heavenly Father has a firm grip on you. His promises are *tenaciously* true. He will answer you when you cry out to Him.

All for His Glory!

Gina is grateful to God for giving her Jesus, through whom she intentionally seeks to live daily. She is a wife, mother, daughter, sister, friend, nurse, mentor, speaker, and now author by the grace of God. Her heart is to reach other beautifully broken people and teach them about God's amazing grace.

Married for twenty years to her soulmate, Jason, they have five kids: Kevin, Lincoln, Julie, Jordan, and Lia, all of whom have drawn her closer and closer to the foot of the cross.

She says, "Raising kids is a labor of love, and God is raising me right alongside them; with each one of them I continue to learn more and more the unmeasurable depths of His love."

She would love to connect with you and hear where you find yourself in the most incredible love story ever told. Life is for more than surviving!

All for His Glory!.

Stephanie Enger-Moreland

Advocacy Equals Tenacity

After facing years of external barriers and internal resistance, I made a judgement call to reach out to a local county council member's assistant about the barriers a client of mine was facing regarding housing. It was a last-ditch effort in sending a strongly worded email. I, with my colleague, had been in this fight for three years. We were exhausting all measures to work a system that was hard to navigate. But the judgement call landed me and a coworker in hot water. Perhaps I should have included the supervisor in the plan, or maybe I thought it was better to "ask for forgiveness rather than permission." Either way, our tenacity won, and I was determined to make headway if not for my client but then for others experiencing the same struggles.

Advocacy for myself, others, and clients wasn't something I had an interest in. But over time I fell in love with how to make this place, office, or community better for those living in it. It's scary to start advocating, especially when you're not entirely sure how it should go, what to say, or what's the best way to go forward. Plus, it's never easy; it can take years, or even decades, to make a lasting change, but I've learned to be tenacious in my advocacy and continue. The last I heard, the client was still struggling to find ample housing.

In 2013 I started out in nonprofit advocacy work as a program associate. My responsibilities included coordinating an annual lobby day, setting up a legislative reception, and keeping up on government policy. Talk about a big gulp! As a young twenty-something I had no idea where to even start. However, I had the organization's Executive Director, Ellen, in my corner. To this day, ten years later, I credit her for showing me the ropes in advocacy. She's been to local government, state legislature offices, and Washington DC to explain what and why certain policies are needed. When I sat in my first committee hearing in Jefferson City, Missouri, my veins felt electric. I watched Ellen and other volunteers testify on behalf of the Victims Economic Safety and Security Act (VESSA), a law to protect those in domestic violence situations with unpaid time off to seek medical attention, file orders of protection, and attend court hearings, to name a few. I witnessed firsthand what advocacy is about, as each person had the tenacity to testify for victims. I loved every moment of it. The hearing was in 2014, and the law was finally passed in 2021. As I said, change takes time.

Later I witnessed one of my favorite examples of advocacy and speaking up, or having the tenacity to step forward, in my former manager, and now friend Lisa. In a staff meeting one morning, she listened to our grievances about some challenges we were facing. As she took notes, she said, "I'll kick that beehive, don't you worry about it." Kicking beehives can be painful, and you could get attacked, but you're going to start a storm no matter what. She was about to challenge the norm on behalf of her team.

From then on, I looked at life differently. I was going to "kick beehives." Advocacy wasn't just for policy change but how I could shift things in the workplace, at home with my family, or in our local community. Having the strength and courage to advocate takes tenacity, as well as understanding what could happen from getting the answer "no" or how it could shape your future.

At one of my jobs, I oversaw a territory that was mostly considered rural. I spent the greater part of three years in the outlining areas getting to know parents, school administrators, and volunteers. I was at times more than an hour and a half drive from suburban St. Louis meeting with families. They voiced their frustration about programs that were too far to access. They wanted to be included in the planning, they wanted programs offered closer to them, and they felt disenfranchised. At a time when my role was merely entry-level, I decided they needed a voice within the organization. I crafted an email to the director of the programs area asking to review how much programming was in the rural area and asking how to change things to make them more included. This director had been with the organization for more than twenty years; truly, I didn't think at the time she knew who I was—another big gulp. I felt strongly about my volunteers and the families I was working with, and that they needed someone on the "inside" for them. While I got a polite email back of "seeing what can be done," I felt proud to voice my thoughts and advocate on behalf of my volunteers and families. Since then, my perception of people in rural areas and the struggles they face in their communities has changed.

During the pandemic, I dug in my heels and got emotional when my executive director was considering opening the building to clients. I thought it was far too soon. "My husband has a heart condition," I explained. I stood firm and wasn't willing to risk his health by being exposed to a virus that was still in its infancy stage. My family felt threatened, so my calm disposition disappeared. After the director heard the emotion in my voice, the conversation shifted to what I and the rest of the team would be comfortable with going forward. It brought me relief.

Advocacy is about having tough conversations with those around me. I've questioned the rules, pushed back on policy, and said no more times than I can count.

Tenacious women are labeled bossy, having an attitude, or, quite simply, as a bitch. Standing in our convictions and advocating for what we believe is right is far from easy. As a teenager, that attitude got me in trouble sometimes when I was standing my ground on principle. I like to think my tenacity is using my teenage attitude as a force for good.

Recently, over lunch, a friend told me about her board of directors. All meetings are in person, once a month, with no hybrid option, she explained. I said, "That's a lot to expect from members. I personally wouldn't join that board if offered." Not long after that conversation, the idea came up again but this time regarding my organization's board. I melted a little inside. In my mind, this wasn't feasible for working parents. If nothing else, the pandemic showed us the need to be flexible and provide options. After the meeting, I told my boss I disagreed with board meetings being strictly in person, explaining that, as a mom, I needed an option for a virtual meeting. I can pay attention to a discussion on my screen and tend to my son if needed.

I knew I was in a safe space to express my feelings and was happy I did. I would have completely shut down with other supervisors I've had. Perhaps it's age or maturity, or I've realized I come first as well as my family. Advocating for myself is a priority, and my tenacity helps me speak up every time.

It never gets easier to speak up on behalf of yourself or others, especially if there is resistance. It's easy to get frustrated, discouraged, and give up. It's not a race but a marathon; with each mile you pass, you slowly start making headway.

I look back at the women who came before me. My grandmothers were both homemakers, raising families during a time when women were fighting for equal rights and shouting from the rooftops. I think about the opportunities I have had, and the times I've stood up to take a stance or voice an opinion to someone who disagrees. I think about the times I've said no to a policy that could harm my family and me. I have no doubt my ancestors would be proud of me. I wonder if there was ever a time when they went a little against the grain, or maybe kicked a beehive or two?

In all these moments, I was determined, steadfast, and knew in my gut what I believed to be right—not just for myself but those I was working to assist. I have since moved on from the previous organization where I was on the hunt to change housing policy, but it brought me to another thing I have investigated within the community: affordable housing.

Do not let fear drive you away from speaking up or speaking out. You never know who is going to benefit from the gesture. You don't know whose world you might change for the better. Tenacity and determination come from within, from the strength of the women who came before us and were unable to speak on their own behalf. I carry this every time I make a move for myself, my family, or my community.

In 2017, Senator Elizabeth Warren was voted by her peers to stop speaking during a confirmation hearing. During the exchange, the Senate voted to silence her. Senator Majority Leader Mitch McConnell explained why the vote was needed, but Senator Warren was not going to stop even after being warned. I like to think of Senator Warren as a kind of partner in crime: "Nevertheless, she persisted."

Stephanie Enger-Moreland is a #1 bestselling international author and a nonprofit executive. She is Chief Development Officer for Kids In The Middle, a mental health agency that supports children and families through divorce and separation. Her career experience has focused on volunteerism, programs, advocacy, and fundraising. Stephanie is an unapologetic guilt-free working mom; it's where she feels most creative. She is a native St. Louisan, born and raised. She earned her master's in Nonprofit Administration from Lindenwood University in 2013. Since then, she's been lending her expertise to support organizations helping those in vulnerable populations.

Stephanie and her husband, Chris, reside in Fenton with their son and two dogs. She is a "bonus" mom to two older daughters. When Stephanie isn't trying to figure out how to change the world, you can find her catching up on all of her favorite housewives or sitting back watching the chaos of her home.

Her chapter is dedicated to her mom, grandmothers, and the women who came before her..

Vidya Thandra Satyanarayana

Fueled by Tenacity, Driven by Determination

"Arise, awake, and stop not till the goal is reached."
– Swami Vivekananda

Born and brought up in southern India with limited opportunities, I always dreamt about being happy and successful, but I didn't realize that figuring out how to achieve them would be the bigger challenge. My name is Vidya. I went from being a business graduate to a stay-at-home mom, to challenging myself to get back to being financially independent after a decade-long break, and I am happy to be currently working as a successful IT professional. Growing up, I was around a lot of strong personalities who inspired and motivated me to approach life with determination and tenacity. Here I am sharing some of the experiences that have molded me to be who I am today. Are you ready for the ride?

Tenacious Little Girl: Beginning of My Musical Journey

As a little girl, I loved the south Indian melodies sung by my mom and grandma. Their passion for Indian classical music inspired me to start singing. By the age of five, I had already gained a good reputation in my neighborhood for being a fast learner and a promising singer. I wanted to sing like my mom and grandma and quickly learned the value of approaching new challenges with determination.

When it was time for me to enroll for formal training in Indian classical music, music teachers who by now already knew about me approached my parents to take me in as their student. That marked the beginning of my journey into Indian classical music. I became more and more confident with every event I performed, won numerous competitions, and carved a name for myself.

I remember one specific competition where I competed in two categories simultaneously, after several hours of rigorous training. I was nervous to be competing against some of the best talents. As the results were announced for the first category, I was so confident that I would win, but I came in third. To say I was disappointed was an understatement; this win meant the world to me. Before they announced the results for the next competition, I decided to walk away. I felt defeated even before the second category results were announced. I remember crossing the road with my dad and feeling so low. My dad was trying to cheer me up by saying that it was a very competitive event, and he was proud of me for winning third place. I still wasn't convinced. We had walked far away from the venue, but I could hear the voice of the announcer. Suddenly, I heard my name: "Vidya. First place." My dad and I looked at each other, laughed for a second, and ran back to the event venue, where I stood in front of more than a hundred people clapping for me. I made it, at last! I was barely able to catch my breath and had my brightest smile. My dad stood at the back of the crowd cheering for me and sharing the same big smile. That scene is sealed in my memory forever. But it also taught me a very valuable lesson: Give your best and keep fighting for it, but don't feel defeated before the results are in. Keep your chin up and hold on to your confidence.

Our house was running out of room for all my trophies, certificates, and medals, but I never stopped. At this point, the setbacks fueled my determination to keep going for more. Failures didn't scare or upset me, and I kept going. My struggles showed me:

- How determined and strong I was.

- My desire to learn more.

- Courage to try not while fearing failure.

- Tenacity to keep going and not back down.

Tenacious Teenager: Musical Journey to a Bigger Platform

As I grew older, I started participating in televised music competitions. That was a whole new experience. I saw the world of what goes into these productions: organizing the schedules of countless participants according to the show's themes, organizing the crew and equipment, scheduling judges, collecting prizes for participants, running rehearsals, communicating with about one thousand participants, etc. I went through a couple of rounds in the competition before getting eliminated. I didn't win the ultimate title, but still the experience taught me a lot. I am proud to have competed and knew I gave my best. The grand prize for the ultimate win was an opportunity to sing on an album by a renowned music director. I thought I missed the opportunity. A miracle was waiting to reward my tenacity. A day or two after my program aired, I got a call from a very famous person. For a second, I didn't realize who it was but then quickly understood the situation. One of the promising music directors reached out to the television company asking specifically for my details and called me to ask if I would be interested in singing for his album. I couldn't believe the offer but knew I would do justice to the task. Recording an album in a studio was a new and memorable experience for me. I gave my best and was invited back couple more times for subsequent projects. I am forever grateful and thankful to the music director for recognizing my talent.

At this point, it was not about the success I was going for but the enjoyment of the process. By enjoying each step, I found that the results took care of themselves. I also never took anything for granted. I pursued every opportunity with the same level of passion.

Tenacious Woman: Cracking Competitive Exam

While pursuing one of the toughest competitive certifications in India, my days began at four a.m. to get focused training for the certification exam. After that, I would work for half a day followed by my bachelor's degree classes, and then back to getting trained for the certification again. By the time I got back home, it usually would be late at night. I had to do this schedule without a break. The schedule was exhausting even more because it was around the time my wedding was being planned. Despite the judgements, questions, and challenges, I kept going after my tenacious goal. I was very fortunate to have a supportive fiancé (now my husband) as well as exceptional mentors who made sure my focus was clear and remained on the outcome. After months of hard work, I aced my exam! I cleared one of the most competitive exams while handling all the stress. The tenacity to keep working for this moment was so worth it. It was one of the proudest moments of my life.

This whole experience made me humble and grateful for the people who supported me through my challenge.

Tenacious Artist: Try Something New

I love taking chances on new ideas and experiments. I always try my best to challenge myself to succeed. During a family walk, I came across an art gallery that sparked my attention. I love art but am not trained in the techniques of creating a work of art. But that's the whole point, right? Art is the creative outcome of our thoughts. I walked into the gallery and negotiated with the owner to display my paintings for sale. I rented a space, setting the stage ready for my artistic debut. Then came the big question: What do I do with that space? I have never created art for sale!

I decided to try, though. I bought a few canvases, then thought through an idea to make it work. An idea sparked. I created an abstract artwork using a South Indian traditional design called "kolam" and made sure all my paintings had a story that would spark everyone's curiosity. I filled the space I rented with my artwork slowly, one painting at a time. But soon I noticed that my fellow artists and the owner were impressed with my work and my determination. My most treasured sale was the painting of a pregnant peahen with a little baby inside her womb blended in with my kolam art. Another artist appreciated my work enough to purchase it.

The experience taught me the value of stepping out of my comfort zone and embracing the creative process.

Tenacity as Mindset: Looking Forward

Armed with all the beautiful experiences and a tenacious attitude, I decided to dare a tough challenge—transitioning my career from a non-IT background to an IT job and reentering the workforce after a decade-long break. This is a hurdle that many women fear when contemplating maternity leave or resigning to care for their families—especially for those who aspire to be financially independent. A challenge I assumed was not possible but was stubborn to figure out, and I did. Now I work as a successful IT professional and do speaking engagements around the world, sharing my story to aspiring, determined women like me. A couple of lessons I learned along the way:

- It's not the challenge, it's the attitude toward the challenge that makes all the difference.
- Not all battles are worth fighting. Choose your battle, gear up to face it, and go for it in full force.
- Enjoy the process and celebrate the journey, not just the success.
- Cherish, appreciate, and celebrate the people you meet along the way.
- Smile, laugh a lot, and take it easy.

Always remember, **when you fail and don't give up, you find millions of ways to succeed**.

Vidya is a mom who returned to the workforce after a decade-long break. She holds a bachelor's degree in Business and is also a Certified Chartered Accountant from India. After moving to the United States, raising a family, and defeating all social taboos for women returning back to the workforce after a break, she is now a successful IT professional.

Vidya has been featured in *Forbes*, Fox news, The Women's Foundation of Greater St. Louis, and other media channels, sharing her journey to empower women.

She believes in paying it forward and speaks to groups across the globe on encouraging women and helping them see their power rise. She is also one of the contributing authors in *Intention: The Deconstructing G.R.I.T. Collection*, which became a bestseller across many countries.

Vidya is a trained Indian classical music singer and loves to experiment in mixed media art. Her recent passion includes cooking, photography, and learning new technologies..

Sarah Jamison

Believe Beyond Possibilities

"The most difficult thing is the decision to act. The rest is merely tenacity."
~Amelia Earhart

In my life, I have faced monumental challenges, emotionally charged circumstances, and devastating situations that seemed impossible to overcome. I remember a few years ago sitting on the floor of my closet, staring at the shades of brown and off-white carpet fibers, replaying the events of my failed marriage, and wondering, "How did I get here?" The longer I sat in solace, the picture in my mind became clearer. I've discovered that after quiet reflection and deep soul-searching, I can identify the decisions, circumstances, and/or events that led me to certain situations or outcomes. However, the day I received the diagnoses that would change my life forever, the overall picture did not immediately become clear.

It was 2016, an early Sunday morning, around one a.m. I sat on my couch wondering, "What just happened to me? Did I have a stroke?"

The sensation I felt was like an electrical current had shot from the top of my head down the right side of my face to my right arm. Then my right hand started shaking uncontrollably. I knew I had to act quickly, so I went directly to the bathroom mirror and checked my face: no drooping. I smiled with ease. "Yes!"

My arms felt normal and not weak. "Yes!" I faced the mirror again and said, "I-am-o-k." My speech was not slurred. "Yessah!" Thank God it was not a stroke! But what was it?

I went to the emergency room, and finally the ER physician explained the results of the multiple diagnostic tests. I wondered, "Do I work too many long hours?" "Do I worry too much?" "Am I holding on to negative stuff?" "Um, what time is it?" "I think I can still make the flight."

The diagnoses: multiple sclerosis (MS) and a benign meningioma.

"Oh, wow..." My thoughts stopped.

A few seconds after receiving the news, my dad and my older brother arrived. My mom was at home waiting with bated breath to hear more about what was going on with me. My family knew something major had happened because I was scheduled to leave for a business trip that morning, but instead of boarding an airplane, I landed in the ER.

The doctor continued talking. I tried to listen, but my thoughts shifted to the prognoses and what was next. I nodded and heard myself say, "OK." However, my mind would not allow me to stay stuck on the limitations of the diagnoses, drug therapies, disease progression, possible complications, or the mystery of both conditions. Simply put, it was Go Time for me. I needed to learn all I could about the diagnoses, do all I could to ensure positive outcomes, and release the rest of my healing journey to God. What I knew for sure: the diagnoses would not be the end of my story.

I accepted the facts but not the opinions. The doctors told me that managing MS symptoms would require medication for the rest of my life. They mentioned Eastern therapies for symptom relief. I resolved that I would not be on medication the rest of my life, and that I would live an abundant and full life. I was determined to be the exception and not the rule.

Where did that never-give-up, tenacious spirit come from? The *Oxford English Dictionary* defines tenacity as: "The quality or fact of being determined and persistent." When I think back to my childhood, I realize the *can-do will-do* spirit has always lived within me.

In grade school, I wanted to learn more about running a business. So I created an opportunity to learn from a local business owner. There was a mom-and-pop convenience store across the alley from our four-family flat. One afternoon I approached the proprietors, a lovely couple, and asked if I could work in their store. They obliged me and told me my job would be counting penny candy for the neighborhood kids, and my compensation would be a bag of penny candy. That was at least twenty-five pieces of candy per workday, and to an eight-year-old that was perfect pay for an amazing job. I ran home and asked—or rather begged—my mom for permission. She gave me her blessing. My lessons in small business operations began the very next day. Win!

Then when I was eleven years old, I wanted to learn how to drive. Back in the day, cars had to be moved on certain days from one side of the street to the other to accommodate street sweepers. Instead of waiting for lessons, I asked my dad if I could move our family car on the designated days. To my surprise and without much convincing, my dad said "Yes!" That was the beginning of my driving lessons, and by age fourteen I was driving to and from church, to visit friends and relatives, and to run errands. (Kids, don't try this now!)

The list of hurdles, challenges, and stubborn persistence are themes that have been present throughout my life. What keeps me moving toward the win?

Inner Strength
Courage, and
Faith on Steroids

So, in 2020, when I was faced with what seemed to be insurmountable odds, I activated the power within me and moved into action.

Challenge #1: Benign meningioma, a non-cancerous tumor that arises from the membranes surrounding the brain. Initially my neurosurgeon and I agreed to monitor the tumor with an annual Magnetic Resonance Imaging (MRI). If the tumor didn't grow, no additional treatments would be needed. However, in October 2020, an MRI revealed the tumor had grown. I sought three medical opinions, and each physician provided identical options: surgery, radiation, or monitor the tumor for another year and then choose a treatment.

My Dilemmas: My daughter planned to get married in October 2021, and I was studying for an Integrative Nutrition Certification from the Institute for Integrative Nutrition (IIN). My anticipated graduation was January 2021.

My Decision: Surgery. My neurosurgeon and I scheduled the craniotomy two days before Thanksgiving 2020, in the midst of the pandemic.

My Goals: Recover from surgery and be fully present for my daughter's wedding planning and wedding. Complete the certification and graduate with my IIN classmates.

My Determination paid off. I graduated from IIN in January 2021, and I helped plan and coordinate my daughter and son-in-love's wedding. My baby girl and I danced, and we had a beautiful celebration of love with family and friends. Win!

Challenge #2: Multiple sclerosis (MS), a central nervous system disorder in which the immune system attacks the myelin, the protective covering of nerves.

My Dilemma: I was prescribed an injectable medical therapy that I self-injected three days per week.

My Decision: During the course of the first year, I researched and implemented additional therapies and treatments including message therapy, acupuncture, meditation, heart coherence, functional medicine, nutritional options, supplements, and increased physical activity. I also practiced daily gratitude journaling.

My Goal: Decrease the need for the injectable medication and live the life I envisioned for myself.

My Determination paid off: I changed my diet to gluten-free and vegan-ish (my daughter's term), and over the past several years, my symptoms and flare-ups decreased significantly. Hippocrates said it best: "Let food be thy medicine and medicine be thy food." Now I am living my best vision. My friends and I recently returned from an eight-day trip in Italy. I walked six to ten miles per day, ate authentic Italian cuisine, and delved feet first into the culture. Winning!

My health and life continue to elevate. The key to a life that gets better and greater is to ensure all areas of life are in balance. The first step is awareness of all the things that impact our wellbeing. The circle of life, as illustrated by IIN, identifies the foods "off the plate" that affect our life. These areas include: Joy, Spirituality, Creativity, Finance, Career, Education, Health, Physical Activity, Home Cooking, Home Environment, Relationships, and Social Life.

When these areas are in balance, they nourish our mind, body, and spirit as we journey toward divine health and wellbeing.

My journey to wellbeing has not been linear. What I've learned along the way is that when I set my intention and worked toward the *Win*, my life expanded. Each victory strengthened my resolve, reinforced my courage, and gave me the confidence to rejuvenate and be the best me physically, mentally, emotionally, and spiritually.

Tenacity keeps me looking forward and not looking back because, frankly, I'm not going that way. What I know for sure is that I did not acquire perseverance on my own. I stand on the shoulders of my ancestors known and unknown, my parents, and other chosen mentors who taught me to keep moving forward, grasp the thing that seems impossible, persist to triumph, and uplift others along the way.

My faith has taught me there is no looking back, to press toward the mark, and to look inward, onward, and upward. Maya Angelou said it so eloquently: "Like air, I'll rise."

I believe God, the Universe, or however you identify a Higher Power, has given us everything we need to overcome and soar. Tap into your inner strength, be curious, be courageous, be determined, be persistent, believe, and live an abundant and prismatic life. You Win!

Sarah Jamison is a consultant, facilitator, and coach who is passionate about helping others achieve personal and professional goals. Her entrepreneurial pursuits coalesced in 2015 when she founded SLP3, LLC, a consulting, training, and coaching organization. Over the course of her corporate career, Sarah held several leadership and executive roles in Human Resources. In 2021, Sarah also launched Elevate Health and Wellbeing LLC, a health coaching practice based on integrative nutrition concepts.

After more than twenty-five years in business industry, Sarah chose to transition to education. She is currently Director of Career Education for Saint Louis University Chaifetz School of Business. Sarah also serves on the Finance, Operations and Human Resources Board Committee of the St. Louis Area Diaper Bank. The Diaper Bank works to end diaper need and period poverty.

Sarah's passion, patience, and persistence fuels her desire to inspire and help empower others to flourish and live their best vision.

Meredith Knopp

Building Tenacity: The Heart Behind Thick Skin

"Have you always had thick skin?" someone recently asked me. "Was it something that you got through the military, or have you always been able to take a lot of punches and keep moving forward?" As I thought about my response, two things became clear: First, I have had many opportunities to build perspective, and unexpected challenges that have created my thick skin; and second, that I have had a lot of support during these perspective-building experiences. This combination of challenges, people, and perspective are the building blocks for my tenacity muscles. My greatest times of growth happened during my most intense challenges.

As a child, I don't remember being called "tenacious." However, I do recall being described as determined and ambitious. I never gave up when it came to things like sports or music. I always had an inner drive and desire to win —to prove myself and to make my parents proud. I played many sports and always gave 110 percent, but I really focused on tennis and softball. I succeeded in both, including making the Softball All-State team during my senior year, with the second highest batting average in the entire state of Michigan. Coming in second became a critical lesson for me. My coach was so excited and proud to tell me the news, but all I could think was, "Second place?!" I was furious that I could have had that coveted #1 slot if I had played in the *one* game I didn't play in because the coach wanted to give me a rest and let another girl start. I was *that* determined, and I thought it mattered. He told me I should be proud and enjoy the moment, that no one would remember who was number one (or two) a year from now, and to understand that "You don't always need to be number one to be a success." Of course, being a seventeen-year-old who *clearly* knew everything, I didn't listen to him, nor did I want to. It wasn't until many years later that I recognized he was giving me life advice, not just high school softball advice. He was the best coach and mentor— who inspired my grit, determination, and passion for the sport—but also helped shape my perspective on life in a way that I could never truly repay. This was my first real life lesson on tenacity.

After graduating from college, I entered the United States Army as a 2nd Lieutenant. I went through Airborne School, and was sent to Fort Hood, Texas. Nine months after I arrived, my company received deployment orders to Bosnia, in support of their first elections following the 1995 war. My platoon was the only United States military presence in the Russian sector of Bosnia during the elections. This was an *interesting* situation for a twenty-three-year-old *woman*—leading troops and working with Bosnian and Russian military leaders who did not want to recognize or work with a woman. Thankfully, I was blessed to have a platoon sergeant and squad leaders who had my back. When these leaders told me to my face in a very stern tone (which I clearly understood even without the aid of a translator) that they "did not deal with women," my platoon sergeant and squad leaders responded, "Well, she's in charge, so you'd better learn." This critical moment in my young military career reinforced the importance of trust, respect, and perseverance in having the ability to face a short-term difficulty by focusing on the long-term goal.

These tests of my tenacity occurred *repeatedly* during my military career and helped me through my greatest challenge: serving in Korea as Company Commander. I took command, full of determination and optimism, laser-focused on working with my first sergeant to make us the best company in the brigade. On my second night in command, my phone rang around two a.m. One of my platoon sergeants, also a woman in command, told me that a soldier had broken curfew, was drinking underage, and that she was taking him to the troop medical clinic for a blood test. This was standard procedure, and she would call me back in an hour. An hour later I answered my phone, and the voice on the other end shouted, "She's been shot! She's been shot! My God, she's been shot!" I had no idea who was on the phone, who they were referring to, or even where they were. I would soon learn the horrific details of the murder of my beloved platoon sergeant at the hands of an intoxicated soldier.

The next twenty-four hours were spent working with United States and Korean authorities to apprehend the soldier. I drove to their installation to try to find the answers, words, and ways to make sense of a situation that defied explanation, with no manual on how to respond. Just seven days earlier, I'd given a speech to my company saying we were going to be better than ever. Now, here I was, giving a eulogy to a standing room only church in Seoul, Korea. I stood in the back of the church before the funeral, candidly sharing my emotional struggles with my battalion commander. I asked, "What in the world can I possibly say? Why did this happen? I don't have any answers, only questions." Holding back her own emotions, she gently smiled and said, "None of us will ever know why this happened. All I know is that you are here right now because you are the one that will help this unit through this. God put you here in this moment in time. So take a deep breath, Commander, and go lead." At the time, her words provided little, if any, comfort; but just as my softball coach years before, she spoke the words I needed to hear. She taught me a life lesson to build me up to my next level of tenacity: keep moving forward, even in the face of seemingly insurmountable odds.

After the military, I worked in the for-profit sector for five-plus years. Then I had the honor of serving at two wonderful nonprofit organizations in St. Louis, where I learned so much from great leaders, teams, and communities. In February 2018, I was named the president and CEO of the St. Louis Area Foodbank. This incredible organization has a phenomenal network of more than six hundred partner agencies (food pantries that distribute food across twenty-six counties), donors, volunteers, board of directors, and, yes, inspiring and amazing staff who care deeply about our community. The past five years have been marked by flooding, a global pandemic, more flooding, and now a very uncertain economic situation and inflation—a challenging era for our community, region, and country. When the pandemic hit in March of 2020, nobody knew what was going on, what to do, or how to protect themselves. Businesses closed their doors, and the number of people needing support skyrocketed. There was no playbook, no instructions. Everyone was in this together, yet completely on their own.

Our goals at the Foodbank were simple: keep our team safe and keep the doors open. Sometimes the simplest of goals can be the most difficult to achieve. The pandemic tested us in ways that we never imagined and made us find answers to questions we never knew we would be asked. This experience also helped evolve how I define tenacity, because leading through a pandemic required patience, creativity, and analytical thinking. Our team accomplished amazing things, and they showed true grit. One of our drivers, who was among those most exposed to the public, and thus the virus, told me one morning that although they were scared, they "had to keep showing up because people were counting on me." Their grit was a powerful example of the mindset, sense of purpose, and true heart that is demonstrated daily by the incredible people that serve the St. Louis Area Foodbank.

Throughout my life, God has placed people in my life to teach me lessons, to help me grow, and to help me navigate the most challenging of situations. Life is filled with lessons to learn; some will be harder than others, and sometimes life gets messy. You will make mistakes. You will fail. You will get hurt. However, I have also learned that, just like when I would get hurt playing sports, injuries eventually heal, and only scars remain. Scars tell a story about our lives, our journeys, and what we learned from each experience. You won't always have visible scars from life's challenges, but every time you face difficulties, remember that it's how you choose to face those challenges that defines you. Your perspective, your ability to remain positive, and having the courage to face everything and anything that comes your way can make the difference in how a situation plays out.

The question "Have you always had thick skin?" is easier to answer than I realized.

Yes, I have always had thick skin, but there is no "secret sauce" to it. Being tenacious is a journey—and your tenacity will grow and evolve as you do, if you have the courage to always keep your eyes and heart open to the people around you. These people are in your life for a reason; never be afraid to lean in and learn and grow from them. They are the ones that will touch your heart, shape your perspectives, and help you become more confident and comfortable in your own skin, no matter how thick or thin it might be.

The only quote that hangs in my office is one from Nelson Mandela, and it epitomizes my continual journey toward building tenacity: "Do not judge me by my successes; judge me by how many times I fell down and got back up again."

Meredith Knopp is a US Army Veteran who has served as President and CEO of the St. Louis Area Foodbank since 2018. Named one of the Top 25 Most Influential Businesswomen in St. Louis in 2020, and a St. Louis TITAN 100 in 2023, she believes that her experiences in the military, leading big-box retail stores, and serving in the nonprofit sector have provided a unique set of both skills and perspectives that she hopes to share with future leaders. Meredith has served as a member of the Missouri Veterans Commission since 2018, and as Vice-Chair since 2021. She believes in the power of collaborating with leaders across the region, always paying it forward, and enjoys opportunities to speak with and mentor young women leaders. She coaches softball, working to build both skills and strong character traits in young girls, like her coaches did for her when she was growing up, and lives in St. Peters, Missouri, with her husband, Ken, and their daughter, Abigail.

Joani Alsop

Faith That I'm Already Me

In-stability and Confidence

I've always been tenacious: smart, determined, pioneering, persistent, strong. Last year when I experienced sudden concurrent life changes, I felt the wind right knocked out of me. I felt I had lost my tenacity. I didn't realize that wind was my spirit, and thought I would soon be back, full steam ahead. I was thinking of tenacity in the usual way, as a doing/goal-achieving thing. And I thought I was not "doing" well. I wasn't where I wanted to be.

Then on yourdictionary.com I found an unexpected definition of tenacity: "the quality of bodies which keeps them from parting; cohesiveness, the effect of attraction." I sensed a different feminine energy and saw another side to tenacity, and recognized when my tenacity was no longer a strength. In the trauma of these sudden changes, I became disconnected from my authentic self and in how I was seeing myself, by holding onto situations that weren't working well for me.

Yet, when the events occurred, I heard a clear voice inside telling me these situations weren't aligned with my highest good and that's why they were falling away. I slowly began to move through the pain from the disconnections to reach my true Self, and to reconnect with strengths and talents I had minimized. I was viewing myself through others' eyes and seeing "not enough" instead of seeing my own strengths and leadership.

I now see "instability" as stability within. I see "confidence" as faith in me, part of my inner tenacity to restore connection and cohesiveness with my True Self as my true tenacity.

Not Just a Girl

I grew up as the oldest of four in a first-generation middle-class suburban family to parents who were about to adopt a baby boy when I arrived, which was a big surprise as the firstborn girl in a family legacy of boys.

I was seen as "just a girl," with no expectations for me other than getting married and raising a family, maybe working for a short time in one of the few basic professions my mother had to choose from: nurse, secretary, or teacher.

But I was a pioneer and explorer, with the heart of a teacher. My early roles in sales and leadership showed me the importance of having the courage to speak, of listening to and inspiring everyone on the team, working together, and having fun! I loved nurturing the growth and development of those with whom I worked, especially women. For a women's conference with Riane Eisler, author of the *Feminine Face of God*, I curated a women's art showcase, which brought insight into the beauty of women's spirits and began my journey of reclaiming the fullness of my feminine identity.

My life changed significantly during a period when I faced most of the major life changes one can experience. My parents died unexpectedly from short illnesses just a few years apart. My amazing manager moved to a new city, and I was promoted three weeks after my mom passed. My marriage fell apart in the midst of caregiving and grieving my parents' passing, and I moved. Then my uncle, who had been a rock in my life, died unexpectedly.

After my aunt died several years later, I earned my master's degree in Organizational Leadership and Development. I felt called to focus on women's leadership development, especially evidence-based positive growth practices, instead of barriers. I held consulting, coaching, and leadership roles while supporting my brother and young nephews during my sister-in-law's sudden cancer diagnosis and passing.

Owning My Growth

Throughout that period, I developed innovative and nationally recognized programs, led larger teams, facilitated workshops, and coached managers and senior leaders. I loved the work, my colleagues, and my clients. I supported many people in transitions to the next phases of their life, empowering them to see their strengths. I applied my education and professional experience in understanding women's unique needs to become fully expressed humans, and was inspired to see so many talented tenacious women blossom into the amazing leaders they are meant to be.

Coaching and leadership development are essential to upleveling systems and empowering all women to have the freedom, sovereignty, and agency to develop our strengths and live our purpose, to be all we're uniquely born to be and not be "just girls." Women show immense tenacity in navigating systems that weren't made by or for us, while leading homes, families, communities, teams, and companies to grow, prosper, and thrive. There's no "just" in any of that!

Faith in Me

My recent transition time allowed me space to realize an essential insight: that I am already whole and am evolving into who I'm meant to be, much like the acorn becoming the oak tree. With faith in myself, I am able to drop the doubts and self-criticism that aren't my authentic voice and aren't helpful. I hear the difference between the voice that's strengthening me or weakening me. I can choose growth without feeling less as I am. I know I'm continuing to evolve into all of who I already am within and allow mySelf to unfold. I looked outside myself for too long, to "experts" and role models, for guidance to help me find the right path to where I belong, rather than listening within, knowing I already belong. This transition time became a blessing in learning who and what to trust: my higher Guidance and higher Self.

It's like a puzzle, bringing pieces of mySelf back together, noticing when some of the pieces didn't belong in my picture. I'm grateful to long-time friends who reflected pieces of my true Self that I had forgotten back to me. I'd thought those parts of me didn't matter or had minimized them to make others feel comfortable. These friends reminded me of my value and of the amazing power of love and acceptance to heal. It's truly been a process of returning to life.

Owning My Identity

My identity isn't the labels I accept or reject, or the titles and positions I've held. It's something deeper, felt within, a wholeness untouchable by others' opinions or judgments, something I always wanted to connect with: faith and confidence in myself. I am enough. I am good enough. I feel it, believe it, know it. Life has brought me to this point, and I am grateful.

As I reflected on how I've successfully navigated other significant changes in my life, some actions stood out as supportive, and other actions hindered my ability to integrate these changes. The times when I settled, self-sacrificed, or tenaciously strove to achieve a certain outcome proved to be unsustainable. When I leaned into learning, with curiosity, faith in mySelf, and a willingness to check within for an intuitive "yes" to opportunities, try new things, and share my best, I expanded my being and opened the same space for others. Those actions were in alignment with the inner essence of who I am.

Embodied Strength

When my life changed for the second time with the sudden end of a relationship and work role, this time I stopped. I did my inner work. I took time to sleep, to feel, to grieve and release what was gone, to learn to let go, to drop attachments to outer labels, and to find within me space, grace, and love. I learned to reconnect to my vital energy and collaborate with it. I am grounded, centered, open, happy, sound.

I've rediscovered amazing gifts, such as my relationship with a great body that's always been my friend and guides me, when I listen, to make good choices to feel my best. As a young girl I loved dancing ballet, which teaches tenacity. Dedicated practice trained my body to attain the positions, gain the strength to jump, the balance to spin, to stay centered and focused, and the peripheral awareness to be a good team member and move in unison with others, along with the courage to be seen in several solos. I danced for more than twenty-five years to stay fit and keep my spirit strong. I now practice yoga, Zumba, and strength training, and I'm grateful for the strength and wisdom my body provides.

Owning My Strength

My strong intuitive sense, also anchored in my body, guides me to what's right for me, to be mindfully present, listen deeply, and ask thoughtful questions, which supports my coaching. I have the tenacity to trust the Spirit within me, to be happy now, no matter what, being present to all that life offers!

Tenacity Is for You

Everyone's journey is unique. While I was persisting in mine, I didn't really know what I was persisting for. Now I know it's not for what but for whom, for me, my life. What's worked for me is to have the courage to listen within and trust my body's wisdom, my heart's love, my soul's guidance, my spirit's goodness, and the essence of who I am as a woman, to partner and co-create with Spirit. I trust that something within me is guiding me and will be fulfilled. I trust that something within you is also guiding you to become who you are here to be.

Tenacity for Life

I recently accepted a role providing leadership coaching and consulting for mid-size organizations, and I look forward to supporting organizations and people to truly thrive. I continue to empower amazing women to claim their unique wholeness and ability to evolve into the fullness of who they're meant to be, to engage their tenacity to live the life of their dreams and thrive in their lives, as I do the same. I'm excited to inspire people to live from happiness from the inside and share it with the world, to collectively create a world that works for everyone. I believe this is why we're here. I have faith we're already and always becoming who we're meant to be!

Joani is a coach, consultant, facilitator, and leader experienced in leadership and organization development, coaching, and career development, focused on empowering people, especially women, to lead with love from authenticity and joy.

She is a Senior Consultant with AAIM Employers Association. Prior roles include FOCUS St. Louis Director of Learning and Women in Leadership Program Facilitator, Coach/Consultant with a global consulting company, and Associate Director, Career Management with Maryville University.

Joani holds a BS in Business Management and MA in Organizational Leadership & Development. She completed her coach training as a Master Business Coach and Performance Leadership Coach.

She serves on the International Coach Federation St. Louis Board as Diversity, Equity, Inclusion and Belonging Director, St. Louis Organization Development Network Board, and is a member of SHRM Lewis & Clark.

Joani is Dare to Lead trained, a Certified Happiness Trainer, Certified in the Birkman and MBTI, and experienced with fifteen leadership assessments.

Colonel Laurel "Buff" Burkel, US Air Force (ret)

One Tuff Bird

Get in shape for your life. …you never know when you might need it!

I sat across from the neurosurgeon that October day in 2015 at Landstuhl Regional Medical Center, our US military's premier medical facility in Germany. He talked about consultations with colleagues and the best way to treat my severely broken neck. I sustained the injury two days prior in a NATO helicopter crash in Kabul, Afghanistan, that killed five people—including two US Air Force members who had worked with me—and injured four more, including me.

My thoughts wandered: Phyllis and Greg were gone; my jet fuel–soaked uniform was cut off me immediately after the crash; I was literally whisked away from my advising role with the Afghan Air Force and flown to Germany less than twenty-four hours after the crash; I had a small bag of my belongings with me but no shoes, no uniform, no credit card; I was bruised, bashed up, and wearing a neck collar; would I ever drive my beloved BMW Z4 roadster again?

The doctor prescribed installing a halo to stabilize and provide traction for my broken C2 vertebra. Known as a "hangman's fracture," it's the same injury that Christopher Reeves—of Superman fame—had sustained a few years previously. Then they recommended a fusion procedure to address the damage to the disc between my C5 and C6 vertebrae…

wait, *what*? At age forty-seven, I'd never had an IV or a surgery in my life. Heck, getting a cavity filled was a scary medical procedure for me. The idea of drilling holes in my skull to install screws to keep the halo frame in place, and that they would cut my neck open to move my windpipe out of the way to get to my damaged disc, was beyond overwhelming.

I had faced physical challenges in the past—playing high school football with the boys, maintaining AF fitness standards throughout my career, a touch of pneumonia early in my AF career, a scratched cornea on a deployment, and a torn ring-finger tendon a month before the crash. These were minor compared to what now lay before me: the toughest and most daunting health/fitness challenge of my life.

How would I make it through this terrifying and disorienting experience with a body, heart, mind, and soul still reeling from what had happened? Answer: with tenacity in my approach to my fitness.

I am never, ever in the shape I want to be in, but I am *always* trying to get there. My survival in that crash and subsequent recovery would have either not happened or been less successful if I didn't have a tenacious, lifelong approach to fitness. Tenacious fitness is a foundation of the recovery journey I continue to walk to this day.

Do you have a tenacious approach to your personal fitness?

If so, outstanding! How can you further leverage that to live your best life, keep after and get closer to that shape you want to be in, be more resilient when life throws something tough your way, and share your tenacious fitness with others to ignite or rekindle theirs?

If you don't have a tenacious approach to fitness, I hope I can help get you started toward getting in shape for your life!

To begin with, tenacious fitness has both short-term and long-term components.

Short-term tenacious fitness is pushing through that immediate workout or fitness activity—see it through!

During the five days I spent in the hospital post-surgery, every time I went to the bathroom, my brother (who the Air Force flew over to be my nonmedical attendant for the first two weeks of my recovery) and I would take a walk. We gradually increased the distance, and by the time I was discharged, we were taking ten to fifteen-minute jaunts around and outside the hospital. Those walks were an essential building block of my post-crash fitness; making that short-term tenacious fitness contract with my brother maintained and regained my fitness level.

During my conversation with the neurosurgeon, I asked what I could do to regain some semblance of fitness during the three months that I would wear the halo. I mentioned a treadmill, and he matter-of-factly stated that he had had halo patients fall off treadmills. Wearing a halo restricts peripheral vision and balance—not a good thing. "OK, well," I said, "can I ride an exercise bike?" "Yes," said the doc. That's what I did one day shy of a month after the crash; I rode the bike as part of my first post-crash workout!

I also made good use of the gym in my dorm. Doing push-ups (one of my favorite exercises) in a halo was not a good idea, but I could do planks—a static fitness pose that worked my core but didn't move my neck area. By the time I left Germany, I was doing over four-minute planks.

I bought an eight-pound dumbbell at the Base Exchange and experimented with some exercises. I did morale trips with the Wounded Warrior Project, the Red Cross, Air Force Wounded Warrior Program, and several friends who lived in the area. We were active; it was Christmas Market time in Germany, and we went to several of them and walked—a lot! I kept moving and didn't just sit in my room feeling sorry for myself. My lifelong fitness approach kept me going.

Nowadays, most every morning, I get up and do a fitness routine in my bedroom. I tenaciously focus on completing each exercise and then move on to the next one. That focuses my mind to let go of outside distractors and focus on my body. When I do that for a bit, I've done a routine's worth of exercises. Do a few routines' worth of exercises over a few days or weeks, and I've strung together a fitness regimen and established a routine.

Short-term tenacious fitness is what I leverage to tackle and complete a workout. It's the voice in my head that says, "Keep going…one more rep…one more mile…one more period…one more yoga pose or stretch."

It's the approach to take when getting ready for that annual Air Force fitness test, the next hockey tournament, a 5K, a triathlon, a CrossFit competition, a special event, or whatever short-term goal you seek.

That short-term routine and regimen is important, but is not, in and of itself, full-on tenacious fitness. Keeping after it, along with other fitness activities, is the foundation of long-term tenacious fitness.

Long-term tenacious fitness underpins getting in shape for your life. This does not mean that you must run, and run hard or long, or push and pump endless weights at the gym. It means you diversify your fitness activity portfolio and never rest in your quest to keep after your best fit self. Be creative and open-minded when opportunities to pursue tenacious fitness present themselves. In the airport? Walk the stairs instead of taking the escalator or elevator. Walk to the next terminal instead of taking the train (if you have the time). Fuel your tenacious fitness with smarter food and snack choices. Get good sleep! Give yourself grace when needed. Find supporters who can keep you going when life is making it harder. Tenacious fitness, like resilience, is not an individual sport!

Nowadays, when I tell people about the crash, they invariably are amazed that I am alive, much less living the active, adventurous life I do. Since that day in the neurosurgeon's office, I've hiked Mount Kilimanjaro in October 2018 (and did my USAF retirement ceremony at the summit!) and have traveled the world to share my story of the importance of connections to resilience. I've learned and actively do yoga, coach a girls' hockey team, and three years ago fell in love with and continue to play ice hockey with fellow veterans and other adults who've discovered the great workout and total fun it can be.

And, oh yeah, I drive my Z4!

None of this would be possible or doable without a lifelong, tenacious approach to fitness.

One important note: Sometimes tenacious fitness means taking a nap or taking a rest. Sometimes it means that life's demands might push you around for a bit. That's OK. Long-term tenacious fitness means you get back after it and after that ideal in whatever way that fits you. You acknowledge and give yourself the grace to know there is work ahead and to never quit. Keep after it and have fun doing it. Be open to and find new and interesting ways to get after your fitness. If the gym isn't your thing—OK, what is? What could be? Yoga, hiking, biking, hockey, pickleball, stretching, quiet time, running, Pilates, cross-training, Peloton, basketball, soccer…whatever fitness pursuit resonates with you to keep you going, get after it! Don't settle for a sedentary lifestyle that doesn't contribute to you being your best you.

Nearly eight years ago, I didn't fully appreciate the miracle it was for me to be sitting across from that neurosurgeon, but I do now. That miracle didn't just happen; I had a lot of help along the way. But I laid some of the seeds for it with my lifelong tenacious approach to fitness.

You, too, can be tenacious in your approach to your fitness. Start short term and carry it through to long term. Keep after it; never stop looking for new and creative ways to get in shape for your life. You never know when you might need it!

Colonel Laurel "Buff" Burkel retired from the Air Force in 2018 and now serves as an inspirational/motivational speaker. She is an Air Force ROTC distinguished graduate, and holds a BS and three master's degrees. Buff is a senior navigator with more than 2,100 flight hours in trainers, F-4s, C-141s, and C-130s. Over the course of her 27+ year military career, she commanded a C-130 squadron and served in a variety of leadership positions, including tours in the Republic of Korea, Canada, and Afghanistan.

Buff is a St Louis Blues Warriors hockey player and serves as the team's Board Secretary. She also coaches the Southern Illinois Ladyhawks girls' hockey team and is a member of numerous professional and service organizations, including the Girls Scouts of Eastern Missouri Board of Directors.

Buff shares the story of her survival and recovery from the crash to highlight the power and positivity of our support to and for each other and its fundamental connection to our personal resilience.

Laura Roeseler

Mind Over Matter

"She believed she could, so she did."

- R.S. Grey

I have fond memories of childhood, from going to school, birthday parties, sleepovers, the beach, playing with friends, and much more. In fact, I have vivid memories of school from elementary school all the way through college. Most of these memories are happy, whether it be the joy of recess in grade school or the excitement of independence and extracurriculars in middle school and beyond. However, one school memory I'm not so fond of is the annual fitness test in PE. You might remember this as the Presidential Fitness Test, which consisted of sit-ups, push-ups, pull-ups, a short run, the "v-seat reach," and a one-mile run.

None of these tests appealed to me, but I could manage them, except the one-mile run. This test was the bane of my existence. I dreaded it for weeks and probably started fearing the next run as soon as I finished the current one. In elementary school, we ran laps around the soccer field and would get an unused popsicle stick as the marker for our laps. Once we had accumulated the appropriate number of sticks—which if memory serves was about twelve—our test was complete. In middle school and high school, we ran laps around the track, and I only ran when the coach was looking. As soon as the coach looked away, this girl was walking. Occasionally, I wouldn't act fast enough, and Coach would call out, "Boyd [my maiden name] you're supposed to be running!" and I would start running again. Needless to say, I never scored above the 85th percentile to qualify for the Presidential Physical Fitness Award, and that was just fine with me.

Running was hard: my sides would stitch and ache with every step. My legs painfully cramped up, and sweat poured down my face. Not to mention that my running pace didn't seem much faster than walking, so why bother when I could get where I needed to go, albeit a bit slower, but without pain and not becoming a sweaty mess? As I grew up, I met people who loved running and raved about the miles they ran and races they did. I was happy for them but thought this wasn't for me.

However, shortly after having my youngest son, Jack, in 2011, I was inspired to give running a try. It was equal parts trying to get in shape following the birth of both my sons and an attempt to claim something for myself. To prioritize my physical health and prove to myself that I could do it. What I didn't know at the time is that this running journey would be just as important to my mental health.

I heard about a running program that said you could go from sitting on your bum to running a 5K in about ten weeks. The basis of the program was incremental intervals of walking and running, and it seemed manageable to me; but on the other hand, why would I subject myself to this perceived torture? What had changed from that little girl who hated the mile run to the woman who thought she could take on a 3.1-mile run? Perhaps it was an increase in self-confidence or maybe it was just my sheer stubbornness?

In any case, I downloaded the application on my phone and started the program during my lunch hour or after work at a local park. Sometimes my husband and two young sons would join me, and other times I would enjoy the solitude as I completed my workout on my own. It was hard, and I anxiously awaited the voice in the app that would tell me it was time to walk. I loved hearing that voice and the little bell that chimed to note the walking interval; and I'll be honest when I say that I dreaded the reverse bell that chimed the start of the running interval. But little by little, those walking intervals became shorter and the running intervals got longer.

A few weeks into the program, I wanted to try to run a mile with no walking breaks. I wasn't quite there yet in the program, but I made it through all the previous running intervals even when it was really hard and there was a fire in me to set out to do something I had never done before. I was thirty years old at the time and had never run a mile straight. I was ready to prove to myself that I could. I called my husband to tell him my decision. He and I have been together since high school, and this man knows me so well. He paused and said, "Babe, I don't think you're ready to do that yet. You aren't there in your program." Now, you might think that is harsh, but I can tell you that it lit a fire in me. I curtly told him, "I am ready, and I can do this!" I hung up and ran a beautiful one-mile route through Forest Park in St. Louis, including up and down Art Hill. I called him triumphantly and said, "I did it, babe! You didn't think I could, and I did!" My dear husband laughed and said, "I knew you could, and I knew if I told you that I didn't think you were ready that it would push you."

Shortly after this triumphant run at Forest Park, I completed my first 5K (3.1-mile race) and ran the entire race, which was a huge accomplishment for me. Next, I signed up for a 10K race (6.2 miles) and went in with the mindset that I would run the first 5K and then after the water station at the halfway point I would walk if I needed. I barreled through the water station and ended up running the entire 10K! When I crossed the finish line of that race, I felt like Superwoman. I told my mom,

"I can do anything I put my mind to!" And I felt it in every fiber of my being. I pushed through those six miles even when things were hard. When my lungs and legs burned, when sweat poured down my face, I kept going. One foot in front of the other.

Since 2011, I have completed countless 5K races on my own and with my two amazing sons, Nick and Jack, several 10K races, and five half-marathons (13.1 miles). I qualified as a Half Marathon Fanatic by completing three of the half-marathons in three months. Has the journey been easy? Certainly not. In fact, during training, my dad was diagnosed with a terminal illness and passed away right before I ran my first half-marathon. It would have been easy to back out of that race, but running was an opportunity to clear my head and focus on me. I had a young family, a full-time job, an ill parent, and so many other responsibilities. Taking time to run outside gave me the clarity I desperately needed. With dad's passing, I became acutely aware of the brevity of life and felt the desire to make the most of mine, including my physical health but, more importantly, my mental health.

You see, my running journey was more about my mental health than my physical health. As a young girl, I despised running and everything about it. But as I pull back the layers of that mindset, I wonder if that loathing was masking something bigger? I think it was. It was a way for a little girl to disguise her self-doubt and lack of self-confidence and tell herself that she just wasn't a physically active person.

When running, I discovered that my brain gave up far before my legs ever did. It was my mind and lack of confidence that slowed my feet down to walking. So I started pushing my brain when I went for a run. When I felt tired and worn down, I challenged myself to run to the next tree or the next trash can. Inevitably, when I made it to that landmark, I set a goal to run to the next. It wasn't easy, but it trained my mindset and brain to keep up with my feet. I was building tenacity within myself not only for the races I've completed but for life. I am now confident in knowing I can do hard things; I know that I can do anything I set my mind to. At times, it may just be one step at a time, but that is all it takes.

Running itself is a beautiful representation of life. There will always be hills, potholes, and other obstacles on your path, but one step at a time you can navigate anything that comes your way. Sometimes you can see the obstacle ahead, and other times it might be invisible, but trust in yourself and rely on your tenacity to help push you forward.

After my first half-marathon, I got a tattoo on my right foot that is only legible to me. It's the word "Believe" from my favorite quote listed at the start of this chapter. Embedded in the word is "13.1," the half-marathon distance. The tattoo reminds me every time I take a step that I can do anything I believe I can do. And so can you!

Laura Roeseler, CFRE is a skilled leader and fundraising professional with more than fifteen years' experience in the nonprofit sector. When her childhood aspiration to attend law school and become a lawyer didn't pan out (after a somewhat cataclysmic realization her last semester of college) she found herself in her first nonprofit job at a youth-based service organization shortly after completing her degree. Since that first job, she has been honored to work at several amazing nonprofit organizations working to improve our community.

She is particularly passionate about equity in healthcare and education and empowering youth in our community. She truly enjoys working with staff and volunteers to help an organization reach its annual organizational goals, and donors to reach their philanthropic goals.

Laura graduated from Truman State University with a BA in History and a minor in French. In 2022, she received the Certified Fund Raising Executive credential. She and her husband, Matt, are proudly raising their two sons, Nick and Jack, in South St. Louis County.

She hopes to inspire other women to reignite and strengthen their tenacity to face all of life's successes and challenges.

Sarah Finley

How Did I Get Here?

I wasn't asking for directions. I was having one of those existential moments where I stop and look around and think to myself, "How did I get here? Here to this spot, this moment, this space in time, how?"

Where was "here," you might ask? Well, driving through Everglades National Park, of course. Isn't that where everyone steps outside their own mind and spends forty minutes rehashing the steps it took to get to this place, alone, in a rental car on one of the hottest days of the year in Florida, driving to the southernmost point of the Everglades just to say they'd been there?

Who does that? Me. I do that.

Even though this probably seemed like a perfectly attainable goal to some people, this was a monumental moment in my life. It represented all the hoops I'd jumped through, all the negative moments in my life that turned out to be good, all the failures that caused me to try again. This exact moment, in the heat of the Florida sun, was a result of all those things, and that made me cry.

I started crying and laughing at myself for crying because I couldn't help myself. I was surrounded by the only place on Earth where this ecosystem exists, a beautiful example of an environment that most of the world will never get to see, and I started crying. The tears were ones of joy and release, happiness, and the gratitude that I could experience this trip.

As crazy as all that sounds, that moment is a happy ending to the journey that started my senior year of high school. One of my favorite teachers gave me a certificate that at the time didn't mean much to me. But, after an undisclosed number of years after high school (because I will not date myself by saying what year I graduated), I finally saw in myself what she had seen all those years ago.

The certificate awarded me the title "Most Improved/Tenacious." OK? I guess I improved that year and she wanted to reward that, but, honestly, I have no clue as to why I was given the certificate. It was stored away in my senior yearbook, and I didn't look at it again until I dug it out before a high school reunion.

I have been called lots of things in my short time on this earth, including stubborn, strong-willed, hard-headed, and, my favorite, loud, but rarely have I been called tenacious. I thought that my refusal to give up was a positive trait, something to be proud of. Most of the time, however, the context in which those words were used was resoundingly negative.

Not to be dissuaded, I have very happily carried those monikers with me like a badge of honor, not realizing that all this time I was using these strengths to push myself through life to achieve goals.

After I graduated high school, I went straight to college. I spent a few years skipping classes and having a great time doing a whole lot of nothing. This quickly came to an end when I was kicked out of school for academic probation. I didn't care, I would figure something else out, I always did.

I worked dead-end jobs, moved out of my parents' house, couch-surfed for a while, and ended up meeting a boy and we fell in love. Not long after we moved in together, he decided he wanted to go into business for himself and bought a restaurant. I was 100 percent against this idea. I begged him to not do this even though it seemed like a sexy idea, but he did it anyway. Not too long after making this huge life decision, I got pregnant.

If you aren't familiar with running your own business, especially in the food service industry, it is a lifestyle. Here I was, pregnant, trying to help in the kitchen of this fledgling restaurant, and it wasn't going well. Oh, I forgot to mention that while this was all going on I was taking care of my aging grandmother who had suffered a stroke and could not speak full sentences. I cooked, cleaned, and cared for her while I was pregnant.

Not long after my beautiful baby boy was born into this world, my grandmother departed it, and so did the restaurant. The stress of losing my grandmother, along with having a newborn and closing our only income source was nearly overwhelming, but I stubbornly pushed through. I helped my then-husband find a new job, and we moved on with our lives.

We moved away from the restaurant, back to my hometown, into a house that my parents owned and right into a divorce. So, there I was, a single mother with no job because my soon-to-be ex-husband packed up his bags and got himself an apartment. What did I do? I kept going.

I started working on the weekends so I could be at home during the week with my child. I swore I wasn't going to fall in love again, but I did. We moved out of my hometown and to Belleville where he bought a house for the three of us. He worked for himself, I worked part-time on the weekends or seasonally to supplement our household income. I took some classes at the local junior college to keep myself busy, not expecting to ever actually graduate college.

Everything was going fine, and then, surprise, I got pregnant with my youngest. It was 2008, and we decided to sell the house because it was not big enough for four people. Perfect timing, right? While the economy took a dive, we packed up our house and moved back to my hometown. He tried to work as much as he could, and I tried to make the money stretch as far as possible. I sold secondhand kids' clothes, dabbled in eBay, and did market research studies to make extra money.

After the birth of my youngest, I stayed at home with my boys and took part-time side jobs. As my youngest got older I kept telling myself that I would go back to college when both the boys were in school full time. When the baby went into kindergarten, I enrolled as a full-time college student for the fall semester of 2014. I was thirty-six years old.

It was time to get the degree that I had always wanted to get. Not the one that I was advised to pursue, nor the one that would make me the most money, but the one that I had always had a passion for—archaeology.

Yes, you read that right. No, I do not carry a whip and I am not a tomb raider, but I am a scientist who has a deep love for all the amazing things people leave behind that give us a rare glimpse into their lives.

So, there I was, a thirty-six-year-old mother of two, back to school full time pursuing a degree in my most tried-and-true passion. I spent the next two years in classes, out in the field, digging in dirt, writing papers, and hanging out with kids fifteen years my junior trying to complete what I had started eighteen years earlier.

I graduated in 2016 with a bachelor's degree in Anthropology with a minor in Archaeology and spent the next five years traveling around the Midwest working on some amazing sites and seeing and doing things I never thought I would get to do. But in true Sarah fashion, everything took a different turn in 2021 when I took a new job that didn't involve field work anymore.

"Why would you stop doing something you love?" is usually the first thing I get asked when I rehash my career to this point. It is a valid question, but the answer is simple: because it is an opening to better opportunities. Up to this point in my life, everything that at the time was negative has since turned into a positive:

- If I had not quit college the first time, I wouldn't have my oldest.

- If I had not gotten a divorce, I wouldn't have my youngest.

- If I had not pursued my passion (against the advice of a lot of people), I wouldn't be in the job I am in now.

- My current job is the reason why I was sitting in the Everglades on a hot morning in August, having an existential moment.

- And to add another turn in my path, I am currently working on my master's degree online, at night, to further my passion.

My journey has never been linear. The unexpected twists and turns are what make it unique. It wasn't until I made those unexpected turns that I realized that I was going the right way. I am thankful for the teacher who recognized my tenacious spirit all those years ago, and I am even more thankful for the fact that, finally, through many different twists and turns, I have recognized it within myself.

Sarah Finley is a 1996 graduate of Highland High School, a 2016 graduate of Southern Illinois University at Edwardsville with a bachelor's degree in Anthropology and is currently working toward her master's degree in Cultural Resource Management at New Mexico Highlands University. In her spare time, she enjoys visiting museums, historical sites, and historic cemeteries as well as working on her family genealogy. Sarah is an accomplished singer and performer at numerous venues in the St. Louis area. She is mom to two amazing boys, Ethan and Andrew, and "cat mom" to three very spoiled housecats: Bitsy, Porter, and Ivy. She lives with her boys and her wonderful boyfriend, Scott, in an almost one-hundred-and-fifty-year-old house. She one day hopes to have her PhD and to visit distant cousins in Europe.

Stacey Lampe

Unapologetically Empathic / Unconventionally Optimistic

"Believe in many things, or even just a few; but be sure that one of those wonderful beliefs is in YOU!"
– Stacey Lampe

Many have a divine awakening; perhaps some feel in their soul that they are meant to do something. Others spend a lifetime trying to figure it out. Some fall into the rhythm of those before them while others break the mold.

We don't get to choose the family we are born into, but we can choose to the make best of any situation we face. I was brought up in a toxic environment. The home vibe was negative, and encouragement was lacking. I grew up where abuse was a constant and codependency ran rampant. No matter how good you did, you should have done better. We moved a lot when I was a kid, and I never really felt that I belonged. It was hard for me to trust others or let people in because I was so often let down. I felt like an impostor, striving for constant improvement, belonging, and a sense of purpose.

Even with the negativity in my early life, there was always this deep desire to help others. I often helped kids at school and in the neighborhood with anything (cleaning rooms, doing their chores, helping with homework, babysitting). This need kept growing. In my early twenties I got a flier in the mail about Leukemia and Lymphoma Society's running program where you raise money and run a full marathon to celebrate. I was already doing charity 5Ks on the regular, so what is twenty-three more miles and thousands of dollars of commitment?! It was a little tougher than I let on, but well worth it. Being able to give some of my best self to others is what brought me immense joy. This desire just kept snowballing into bigger things and belonging to organizations whose missions aligned with my unspoken passion.

If you had asked me what I wanted to be in high school, working in construction would never have made the list. At the time, I didn't know this was a viable option for females, and it wasn't on my radar. Yet people happen into circumstances beyond anything they could have envisioned for themselves, and it isn't always charted out for you. Turns out construction was the outlet that fed into my caring side and opened me up to let others see my true self.

My trajectory had been compromised a few times, so my entry into construction was slightly unconventional. After high school I wanted to join the military and serve our country. When that didn't work out, I signed up for business management classes at the community college. I was working a few different jobs while in school (full-time office manager at a dentist office, part-time waiting tables, and part-time retail).

When the dentist decided to move her practice, I began to look for a new career. Not to date myself, but I was scrolling through the "want ads" in the local paper and came across an admin position for a local general contractor that piqued my interest. Although I did not possess *any* knowledge of the industry, I had organizational, administrative, and communication skills that would benefit any position, and a solid work ethic. Surprisingly enough, I was hired, and thus began my career in construction.

I was put to many tests as I maneuvered through unchartered territories. Some days were wins, and others provided life lessons still with me today. Even as the years passed, I still struggled with the impostor syndrome, so I devoted myself to working and helping others. This cultivated my involvement with NAWIC (National Association of Women in Construction). Being a member of NAWIC strengthened my ability to speak in public, plan and execute events in the community, raise money for worthy causes, give back to those in need, mentor, and be mentored.

Who would have guessed that construction would provide a platform of trust and letting people in? Surprisingly, it did. My mentors came from the construction industry. The strong and amazing females I have met along the way are now my most respected and trusted friends. The way these women who have so much in common with each other instantly spring to action if another sister is in need is truly remarkable.

Often, I get the question "So how did you get to where you are?" I got knocked down, *hard*. Questioned, berated, harassed, spoken over in meetings, and ignored. I've been told I care too much, that the positions I had been asked to fill were a setback in my career. A person had the audacity to tell me that I would never make it in this industry. Yet I never stopped pushing forward, I never lessened my care for others. I turned vulnerability, mentoring, and finding my voice into strengths. I got more involved. I attended conferences, trainings, preached positivity, and grew my network. I learned when to let go and the importance of moving on. And when the industry that I devoted so much to wasn't giving me what I needed, I learned to step back and shift my focus to my family.

I would be lying if I told you there weren't tears, stress, fatigue, long hours, getting overlooked for promotions, and unwanted career moves.

All these trials were shadowed by the positive that was also happening simultaneously. I was fortunate to build a Make-a-Wish© home for a local boy, and to spearhead the construction of a memorial for fallen soldiers at Jefferson Barracks Park. I spent time beautifying neighborhoods and helping at women's shelters, and these are just a few notable charitable endeavors that inspired my soul.

I do care too much, but in doing so I have met so many incredible people and made so many unbelievable memories. I have been blessed to share my story, to have sat on panels and spoken to the crowds, been nominated for and even won a few awards. I have had the pleasure of introducing kids to construction and seen the joy of students receiving scholarships because of work I helped do. Caring too much is one of my greatest attributes, and I am unapologetically empathic.

If I had let negativity consume me early on, I would not be where I am today. If those who were afraid to see me grow were allowed to hold me back, I would be confined or, even worse, silenced. The toughest things to happen to me lead me to the beautiful place I am today. I choose to focus on the positive and spread kindness.

Are there days when the impostor syndrome gets the best of me? Yes. But that means I am still growing in the right direction. The ability to move forward when there is a constant to hold you back and the power to brave the unknowns are true characteristics of a relentless person. Life is full of things beyond our control. It's easy to hold grudges, feel ashamed by destructive experiences, or lose your focus. I challenge you to take the admirable route, own it, strive because of it, learn from it, and most importantly not to lose your voice. Never let go of your core values, and keep surpassing those who doubted you and attempted to dim your light. Choose positivity. Choose to shine.

One day it will all make sense, and you will see yourself the way others have been seeing you. It may take a random note from someone you gave a smidgen of time to, thanking you for the impact you made on their life. Or your daughter telling you how you make her proud, that you are an amazing mom and worker. And your son, dedicating a book to you because you are his biggest fan (and he sees it). Find your *why*. Your core people are what make it all worth it. At the end of the day, however good or bad, I get to leave work behind, go home, and hug my adorable family; this is my *why*.

Remember it is never too late to be your best self, so pull up those vulnerability pants, sing loud, and journey ahead! Even when you feel a mess, I guarantee someone is seeing you as an inspiration. *Be her.* Amazing people are found each day doing incredible and selfless things to help others. Surround yourself with brilliant people who genuinely want to see you succeed. True tenacity is not only the determination to move yourself forward but the strength and force to move others with you.

Stacey Lampe is a proud mother of two amazing children and a wife to a very supportive husband. During the day, she enjoys her position as Project Manager for Kozeny Wagner.

She is an advocate and mentor with great love of the industry. Her passion lies with the ability to leverage the generosity of the construction industry while giving back. She has been an active member of the NAWIC (National Association of Women in Construction) St. Louis Chapter #38 for sixteen years and recently helped start the Women-Build Team, a partnership with Habitat for Humanity. She currently sits on the RUCC (Regional Union Construction Council) for Avid Electric, a woman-owned low-voltage company.

Previous honors/awards include NAWIC "Let's Build for Women in Construction Week" (2023), Nominee for SLC3 Woman in Construction (2023 and 2021), CNR's Top 20 of 2020 Women in Construction, *Constructech Magazine's* Women in Construction (2020), and Make-a-Wish© "Wish Granter" (2018).

Heather McLin

Get Uncomfortable

*Someday I will have to tell my five-year-old that he is named after my
deceased brother. And how that started the seeds of tenacity in my life.
But I'll get to that in a minute.*

Tenacity to be vulnerable

I was choking back tears on what should have been a fun day. When my
tight-knit family gets together it is normally loads of fun! We gathered on a
December day in 2012 to take family photos, but I wasn't having fun.

This memorable day became a pivotal moment in my life. My parents,
three younger brothers with their spouses, and I met Jenny, our photographer,
at the park. I felt so much like a third wheel . . . or ninth wheel, in this case.

With photos of the extended family, you know the drill: one big
group picture, one with all the boys, then all the siblings, now one with
all the siblings and their spouses. I felt so awkward as the lone sibling
without a spouse. To make matters worse, Jenny kept encouraging me to
"act natural."

Why was I so upset?

I was lonely. There's nothing like the holidays to bring that feeling out.

At the park, it hit me how tired I was of being single, and I was
feeling sorry for myself. I was totally choked up, and the photographer

kept saying, "Look natural!" OMG. I was trying, but I was barely holding it together!

In the New Year, I decided to take action. I was going to finally make an effort to date and put myself out there. I had barely dated anyone for the past decade. All the Hallmark movies I'd watched had me hoping that Prince Charming would knock on my door. He never did.

The key isn't going on one date. It's having the tenacity to keep going after the inevitable bad date (and there were many). I almost gave up several times. I got stood up one too many times!

But I kept going. I put together a series of steps to help me stick with it. I remembered trying not to sob during family photos. Finding someone meant getting uncomfortable quite a few times first!

Then, in late August that year, I met a guy. A great guy, who's now my husband. No fairy tale movie, but my own Prince Charming. We are now happily married with two kiddos. If I hadn't been tenacious in my approach to dating, we never would have met.

I dug deep and leaned on tenacity several times in my life, and when I have, it has changed my trajectory. But it does require figuring out how to get comfortable with the uncomfortable.

I had an exercise instructor once yell to the class, "Get uncomfortable!" She was talking about all the squats she was making us do, and encouraging us to embrace the shaking in our legs and the feeling that our quads may split right out of our thighs. This teacher's callout has stuck with me forever. I love that this wisdom applies to everything. What amazing things can come after pushing through the shaking legs (or the equivalent in whatever uncomfortable thing you are doing)?

Committing to dating was a shaky-leg moment for sure. It made me feel super vulnerable. But I didn't give up, especially after bad dates. I've had a few of these shaky-leg moments in my life.

Tenacity to try something new

As I get older, I realize my tenacity is a direct inheritance from my dad.

My dad worked hard, and he wanted that same work ethic for my brothers and me. I saw this in him ever since I was a little girl, but I didn't appreciate it at times. As far back as I can remember, I have been a goal-nerd, like my dad—always wanting to feel the accomplishment of achieving something that seemed out of reach.

The lessons/goals continued through high school and college. My dad made us get jobs and make payments for the cars he provided, along with insurance, gas, and maintenance. This seemed so unfair but was teaching us about bills. After we graduated from college, we discovered that he invested every payment we made and gave the money back to us. My parents were building the scaffolding for me, and this work ethic became ingrained in me; I just didn't know it at the time. It explains my need to keep pushing for new things in my life even when I am scared and uncomfortable.

While at my first job after undergrad, I took advantage of a company perk that helped pay for school and decided to get my MBA part time at night. As if this wasn't uncomfortable enough, I became intrigued by the idea of living in a new place. Picture a world where you have been mostly sheltered your entire life, having grown up in a small Western Pennsylvania town, where all your friends and family lived. That was me. And yet I became intent on this idea of moving away to see if I could create a new life experience and make it on my own.

Through my MBA program, I landed a job at a Fortune 500 company in St. Louis. I moved there knowing literally no one.

After only three years in St. Louis, I found my next role within the company, but it was in Chicago. So I moved again, not knowing a soul. I ended up in Chicago for almost ten years. There were some assignments and roles that took incredible tenacity. The tough assignments led to the most growth, learning, and leadership skills, and opened doors for new things!

During my time in Chicago, I met my husband (see above), got married, and at the age of thirty-seven I was promoted to Vice President while pregnant with my first child.

At the end of 2019, we moved back to St. Louis, just in time for the pandemic. Our family was barely settled when I got pregnant again. Both of my pregnancies were during a period of transition to a big new job at work. This time was even more unusual. I was shocked when my boss told me the company was sending everyone home due to the stay-at-home order. As I stood up to leave, I said, "By the way, I am pregnant, just starting the second trimester." It was surreal. Our second son came in September of 2020, and luckily my husband was allowed in the delivery room by then.

So, my wild idea of "Can I leave Western Pennsylvania?" has led me to a great career, two cities, a husband, and two sons. A life I never imagined when this idea came to me!

"Let life amaze you," a colleague once said. This is another bit of wisdom that has always stuck with me. If you look, there are amazing things happening all the time, even in the midst of hard work and the growth and the uncomfortable. It can pull you out to remember the big picture versus the mile-long to-do list. Life gets busy, and it is easy to get lost in the details and not enjoy it. I try to remember this quote from Gretchen Rubin: "The days are long, but years are short." Both these pieces of wisdom can quickly put perspective back in its place.

Tenacity to be bold

When I was pregnant with my first child, we couldn't decide on a name. Then my husband suggested Jonathan, the name of my brother who died when I was eight and he was just an infant (three months old). It was such a hard thing to go through as a kid (I am sure even harder as an adult). Loss like this forces you to learn about tenacity, how to get through the night terrors and trauma and move on. As soon as Jonathan was suggested, it felt right. It felt bold. We checked with my parents and never looked back.

I love being a wife, a working mama, and raising these two boys with my husband. Since I had my kids later (my friends have high schoolers while my youngest is potty training), I am always hyperaware of how fast things are going and how quickly they grow up. Of course, there are times when they are impossible, but mostly they are amazing and adorable and bring loads of joy to our life. I wouldn't have it any other way.

I want to empower my boys to own their life, to go after their goals and to have tenacity and courage to get uncomfortable. After stories, before bed each night, we say:

Tomorrow, I hope you learn something, I hope you try something new, and I hope you do something nice and something bold.

And I know, when the time is right to tell Jonathan about his namesake, it will be one of my boldest days ever.

During dinner each night, I try to ask the boys, "Did you do something bold today?" This question is for them but also for me. I want to answer the question with a powerful "Yes!" I am so fortunate; my husband and my boys support me and encourage me in any new thing I want to try.

This is my hope for all of us, that we continuously learn, but more importantly that we apply what we learn, and push ourselves to try new things, *bold things*, all while showing people kindness in the world.

So if you are not satisfied in any area of your life, use that as a catalyst to get uncomfortable and try something new! Be open to letting life amaze you. The combination of gratitude and working toward your goals can change your life in ways you cannot predict.

As for me, I am embracing my shaky legs at every opportunity.

Heather McLin is a speaker and marketing executive with more than twenty years of experience. In marketing, she loves finding the connection point with the customer and then amplifying that message. She has a proven track record for testing and implementing process improvements using analysis and data-driven decisions.

Heather is Vice President of Marketing at Emerson for Professional Tools (RIDGID & Greenlee brands). She has worked at Emerson for more than sixteen years, including different business units and various functions.

Heather is very passionate about all things related to goals, marketing, and career development. She is a slow jogger, podcast nerd, and a fan of champagne. Heather has an MBA from the University of Pittsburgh. She lives in St. Louis with her husband and two sons.

Lauren Lakebrink

Be Your Own Expert

I would like to start with my birthday, April 20th. I'm starting here because, as a little girl, I wanted horoscopes to help me fit in. Since this date lands on the cusp of Aries and Taurus, I never fully related to either of the readings. I was frustrated because I wanted something to tell me who I was. Now I realize that not fitting into a box is my superpower. I have taken these question marks and formed my own path. I'm not an expert in anything but my own story. It's never too late to be an expert on yourself.

When I didn't speak the first three years of my life, my parents were concerned. There weren't a lot of resources for kids that didn't fit into the educational "box" of mainstream classrooms. I was diagnosed with a learning disability and struggled with reading, writing, and spelling. This learning disability (LD) has followed me everywhere, and I hated being attached to this label; but now I have accepted myself as I am. Accepting our limitations is just one of the steps toward being our own expert.

My struggles started in second grade. I was already showing signs of being behind at such a young age. I went to a small private grade school, but they didn't have much funding for special students. They tried to help by renting a trailer for the "special" kids that was parked outside, right next to the playground. No child wants to feel dumb or left out, but, unfortunately, I felt all these things. Maybe don't sit an LD/ADHD kid next to the playground? Regrettably, the school's attempt to give me more help wasn't enough, and I transferred to a public school. The twist to this story is that transferring schools meant I needed to be held back and repeat second grade. The transfer set the tone of my learning development. By day, in the public school, I was a second grader, but any religious school or church activity would have kept me one grade above that level. This long-term oversight continuously reminded me of my disability from second grade through college. Ten years of always feeling behind or dumb carved a very deep scar.

As a coping mechanism, I would constantly deny that being held back was my fault. I told everyone that I was held back because the private and public-school curriculums didn't match. Therefore, they were responsible for holding me back. In my mind, I fooled everyone, and I'm fine with living that reality still today. I denied my learning disability daily because I just didn't want it to be my label and I refused to let it define me. I didn't realize I was denying who I was, and I never really learned how to advocate for myself. When high school started, all the private schools merged and all my private school classmates were sophomores, but I was a freshman. Yet again, a daily reminder of feeling dumb.

I remember gaining some confidence in my junior year with an English teacher who was ready for retirement. It was no secret he would nap while we had in-class reading assignments. One day, he gave an assignment I was excited about: a double-spaced, three-page book report on any subject of our choosing. I wanted to do a report on elephants.

This might seem silly to others, but to me, libraries were the worst. The smell of the paper would trigger headaches, and the feel of some paper would make my hands sweaty. However, the elephant book had photos that held my attention, the text was simple and double-spaced, the pages were glossy (which didn't make my hands tingle), and I was interested in elephants. I was so proud of this report because I did it on my own and got it done early. He gave me a B without any notes on why the report didn't earn an A. When I asked, he said in a very annoyed tone, "It's about elephants." I remember my ears getting hot because he said the subject could be anything. I said, "Don't dock me for the lack of your direction." In a private school, this was talking back, but I had a point! This moment made me realize that even when I did what was asked, I still got punished for not fitting into a mold. Even though the grade wasn't adjusted, I was excited to have a B for a writing assignment that I accomplished on my own, and that I stood up for myself.

The biggest challenge of my educational life was taking SAT tests in high school. My score was embarrassingly low. The school's guidance counselor did not help me at all. For someone who also had a disability, she did not offer me any guidance, but just tilted her head with a look that made me feel ashamed. All she saw was my score. There I was, limited to my own brain's functionality without even understanding it or knowing how to work around it. I was beyond stressed out and disappointed in myself. I felt like I'd let my family down. I'm grateful my parents didn't let me give up and that they helped me fill out college applications. I'm so grateful SIU–Edwardsville took a chance on me. I'm now a proud graduate with a Bachelor of Science in Speech Communication with an emphasis in public speaking. I love saying I BS'd my way out of college.

I did well in almost every job I had, but I didn't have much passion for them. I thought I would never be happy because I wanted to change jobs every three years. Then someone said, "Lauren, you are just a talented person." What? Me? Say more, please! I had not thought this way about myself. I discovered I'm talented even though I can't process reading material in the same way as others. What else had I missed about myself? A whole new discovery began after one simple comment. I learned about myself and how I process information. This is what I call my LMC method. Learn how you learn, Make mistakes, and Clarify communication.

To understand how I learn, I must reflect on both my failures and successes. When I think of learning, I think of how my brain accepts and retains information. Just because I hear it once doesn't mean I'll remember. I call this: "Regurgitating information that is required and not interesting." I would often be seen as forgetful or ditzy because the information just didn't stay with me. I discovered my learning method in a college history class. It was pure lecture, and the professor allowed us to have an index card with as many notes that would fit on it with us during our tests. I rewrote my index card five times to keep adding material I thought I needed, but when the test came, I had it all memorized! The best part was that it was an essay test and I could explain in my own words. I wasn't dumb! I just needed to understand how I processed information for long-term knowledge. I started asking clarifying questions with the intent of building out a speech or PowerPoint presentation. This method fulfilled the visual, repetition, and application processes I needed to be successful.

I still struggle or make mistakes with my writing sometimes. On job applications, I wasn't taken seriously because I made spelling or grammar mistakes. I didn't get a position, and in my follow-up feedback session, they said, "I was wondering if you knew the difference between 'there' and 'their.'" I was embarrassed because I do know the difference and was reminded of my disability over one word I didn't even misspell. I've had so many mistakes along my path, and I'm sure I will still make more. Making mistakes is how I learn.

I have a bit too many mistakes to list, but I wanted to get better. I swallowed my pride and asked my management to send me back emails with the errors highlighted in red. I changed my frame of mind and said, "This is how I get better. I need to see my mistakes in red." Boy, did I realize two things: I use way too many commas, and I add too many fluffy words. Outside of taking on a new title of "Comma Queen," I needed to start writing very simply, make bullet points, and remove the fluff. I realized that I write how I speak, and the fluff is added to soften my insecurities. I started stating facts only in my emails and followed up with a personal call to show it's factual and not writing in anger. I saw a huge difference in job advancement, respect, and more opportunities to give presentations. I'm grateful my leadership worked with me and not against me. I'm not sure how much further I would have gotten without allowing myself to make mistakes and be open for constructive feedback.

Clarifying communication is what I consider the cherry on top. I'm able to advocate for myself and what I need to be successful. I need to process what I hear, explain back what I heard, and identify any communication gaps. I ask for clarification if I misunderstand something, and I'm not shy about asking for the definition of a word I don't know. Pretending I understand didn't get me anywhere. I needed the confidence and a chance to grow into the person I am today.

My LMC method is in my DNA. Learn how you learn, Make mistakes, and Clarify communications to be your own advocate. If you can't speak for what you need, others won't be able to either. Be your own expert by being tenacious about yourself. You don't need to fit into a mold, but you do need to mold yourself throughout life.

Lauren Lakebrink is the youngest of three siblings and a proud graduate of SIUE, where she earned a B.S. in Speech Communication with an emphasis in public speaking. With a career spanning twenty-five years, Lauren's professional journey has been a testament to her unwavering commitment to personal and professional growth. Lauren specializes in both virtual and in-person training program development and facilitation.

At the core of Lauren's success lies her tenacious ability for self-growth. The LMC method consists of learning how you learn, make mistakes, and clarify your communication. This transformative approach is underscored by a powerful quote that reshaped her perspective: "The exercise you do is the best exercise." This sparked her passion to identify there is no correct or simple answer in self-discovery. Through the LMC method, Lauren empowers individuals to discover what resonates best for them, fostering their own shimmer inside. Communication, in her eyes, remains the cornerstone of every triumph.

Esmeralda Aharon

Tenacity in Adversity

When I reflect on the word "tenacity," I think of fiercely holding on to the hem of Jesus on March 28, 2003, the day my dearest child was born. Like many mothers, when I found out I was having a child, I was overwhelmed with joy. When the military doctor told me that my pregnancy was high risk and that I should consider terminating it, the last thing I wanted to hear was that the pregnancy could kill me and/or my baby. It was then that I had to take courage and faithfully push forward with my pregnancy. No one was going to convince me otherwise. I dug deep into my tenacity well and drew strength mentally, physically, socially, and spiritually to not just survive but thrive through the pregnancy.

At twenty-two weeks' gestation, I was rushed to the emergency room weak and half-awake, and I knew I had to be strong and controlled to ensure that my baby would survive. As I was hemorrhaging, a dear friend did not ask questions when I called her and requested to be rushed to the hospital. I left the house, which looked like a crime scene, with only a towel secured to control the bleeding. My friend did not even bat an eye when the seat of her SUV was stained with a pool of blood. But when I arrived at the hospital and the nurses rushed out to help me, their looks of surprise were hard to mask. I opened my eyes and shut them again. I was "losing too much blood," they said to one another as they rushed to get me inside. When I was stabilized, the doctor told me that I was in grave danger because of the blood loss and that I must terminate the pregnancy. I persistently said, "no." I had previously gone through multiple miscarriages and had already lost a son, so I knew in my heart and mind that if God wanted my baby, he could take her himself.

When my husband arrived at the hospital, the doctor spoke to him and explained the gravity of my health status and that his medical recommendation was to terminate the pregnancy. My husband asked if they had spoken to me already, and after hearing that they had, he said if I had not granted permission to end the pregnancy, then neither would he. There was nothing else the military medical team could do to help me, so they rushed me by ambulance to Saint Luke's Hospital in Boise, Idaho. Upon arrival, the civilian doctor told me he would do everything in his control to give me and the fetus a chance at survival.

For the next four weeks, with my resilient mother at my side, and with numerous prayer warriors crying out to God for mercy, we tenaciously prayed and trusted that my baby would stay in utero for another day. The chances of survival for a micro-preemie are very slim, and in those years, the medical community considered the survivability rate at twenty-four weeks' gestation. We counted the minutes, hours, and days that my darling child continued to "cook" in my belly.

One day the doctor requested a scan to see the placement of the placenta. Very carefully, the technician wrapped a Velcro-style brace around my abdomen in hopes of stopping the baby from moving around. Of course, my strong, amazing child was having a field day. They discovered my illness was worse than anticipated. The reason for the bleeding was placenta percreta, a life-threatening condition affecting one in about 530 pregnancies. The most severe of the types, placenta percreta happens when the placenta passes through the uterine wall and impacts other organs. Later, they discovered the placenta had attached itself to my bladder, impacting both organs. With the baby in a breech position, every time she moved I bled. During the next four weeks, I received blood transfusions and medicines to increase the baby's survivability rate and to quicken her growth. Through grit, resilience, tenacity, and the grace of God, my baby was born at only twenty-six weeks' gestation and weighed 986 grams.

The night before she was born, my body was completely exhausted, having fought the good fight. It could no longer keep her in utero. Every part of my being knew that I was dying. My body was releasing blood like a spigot, again, gushing onto the sheets of my bed. Before I was taken to surgery for an emergency cesarean delivery, my husband, sons, and mother prayed for me. I said my goodbyes and knew in my heart that I would probably never see them again, but I stayed strong for them. There was no turning back. My body could no longer hang on to dear life. I prayed to the heavens above, and with all humility I cried out to the Lord that I was ready to see Jesus, but that if he would grant me life, I would serve him with every part of my being. I would dedicate my life to the service of others. Then I fell asleep.

When I woke up, I had every possible tube connected to me. The machines were beeping loudly as I was waking from my slumber. Though agitated, I could not scream because of the ventilator; but in my head, I began to sing a verse from Chris Tomlin's song "You Are My King": "I'm alive and well, your spirit is within me because you died and rose again." God was in total control, and if he had allowed me to survive this ordeal, he was going to help me thrive and live abundantly. His purpose in my life was not over. Even while awake, the doctors had told my family I was not out of the woods. I had emptied my blood supply and they had given me fourteen units of blood, enough blood to save forty-two people, as one unit of blood can save up to three lives. If you donated blood in 2003, you might have saved my life!

What happened while I was unconscious and fighting for my life? The doctor told my family that my micro-preemie had a higher survivability rate than I did. They had done everything medically possible, and even if I survived, I would probably suffer from intellectual disabilities and other health issues because of the blood loss and organ repairs and removals. The doctor asked my husband if he knew how to pray, because we needed a miracle. A host of family, friends, and colleagues from all over the world would not accept that I was dying, and they prayed fervently for me. I am told that a Chaplain Assistant gathered our chapel team into the sanctuary and led a prayer on my behalf. My Chaplain Corps family showed tenacity and such determination despite the possible outcome. They prayed with conviction that I would wake up, and I did.

God's plan for my life was not finished, and since that day more than twenty years ago, in gratitude and in keeping with the commitment that I made to him, I have served congregations, food pantries, schools, women shelters, Girl Scouts, marginalized communities, and so many others. Through his grace, I graduated with a Bachelor of Science degree, master's degree, and I am now pursuing a PhD., fulfilling my God-given purpose. My brain is intact! After twenty-six years of military service, I completed my duty to the United States Air Force, and as a retiree I continue to serve women veterans, communities of low socioeconomic status, and immigrants. Even after becoming a widow and almost losing my life to the pandemic virus in June 2020, I am tenaciously placing one foot in front of the other and wholeheartedly relying on my faith for strength, hope, and purpose.

Nothing I have been through has been easy, but my faith in God has propelled me from the ashes and has given me the resilience and tenacity

I needed in the deepest times of despair. And what of the child, you might ask? After going through speech, developmental, occupational, and physical therapies, and having multiple eye surgeries, my daughter is now twenty years old and a junior in college.

When you think about the challenges in life that have brought you to your knees, what skills or practices have helped you push forward even when everything around you looked like chaos? For me, it has always been my faith. I have tenacity because of the one who gives me strength (Philippians 4:13). The research shows that having a spiritual practice improves overall outcomes during adversity and provides meaning and purpose. I also rely on my family and friends. Do you have a faith community and tribe surrounding you when you need them? Life was not meant to be lived in silos. You need community.

How controlled have you been when facing adversity? It is not *if* you will face adversity, but *when* you do; being mentally, physically, socially, and spiritually healthy helps you return to your whole self. Holding onto the hem of Jesus (if you are a Christian), your values, or your faith will help you not just survive the adversity but thrive despite it. Maybe you have not been at the verge of walking "through the valley of the shadow of death" (Psalm 23:4) like I have, but you can still stay the course in your circumstances and be courageous and controlled to pursue your life's passion. Put one foot in front of the other, literally and figuratively. Be tenacious in your faith and in your values. You have purpose!

Esmeralda Aharon is a bilingual Latina educator, and a diversity, equity, and inclusion practitioner at Saint Louis University School of Medicine. She is a combat veteran whose service spanned over two decades in the United States Air Force. She advised leaders at all levels on ethical, moral, and morale issues impacting the enlisted force, and inspired readiness, spiritual fitness, and resilience. As community leader, she holds several board positions and advocates for people of color, veterans, and language access for non-English speakers. She has garnered numerous awards including the prestigious Spirit of the Four Chaplains, Senior Noncommissioned Officer of the Year, LATINA Style Distinguished Military Service, and Adelante Hispanic Lifetime Achievement, among others. She holds a Master of Arts degree in Teaching Elementary Education from Liberty University and is a doctoral student at Saint Louis University. Esmeralda is a doting mother, and in her spare time she travels, hikes, reads, and practices yoga.

Dawn Higgins

Like Mother, Like Daughter

Where there's a will, there's a way, and tenacity is just that: never giving up until the goal is met, or at least knowing when to pivot, move on, and walk away. My mom, Victoria, has never stopped doing what needed to be done to take care of me. I've always admired her resilience, spirit, and her loveable attitude. She is my biggest cheerleader and supporter. While I have always had two supportive parents, the bond with my mom is like no other, and I thank you, Mom, for all that you have done and continue to do. She is my Shero.

I've always been a go-getter. In high school, I wanted to be on the cheerleading squad and the dance squad. I tried out for both teams a couple of consecutive years and never made either one. My freshman year of college, however, guess what? I made the cheerleading team. I realized high school just wasn't my time to be a cheerleader, but it may have been my first encounter with tenacity. Growing up mostly as an only child because I have a brother and we are sixteen years apart, I enjoyed being by myself, but I also wanted that connection with others. So I joined several activities and organizations not just as a member but to serve. Leadership was important, and I took on those roles where I could.

It's funny how you can dream about how your life is going to turn out, and it does not go quite as expected. But God doesn't make mistakes because he has the path set for me. Life has been good to me. I have a wonderful husband and family, a good career, awesome friends, and sorority sisters, etc. My first career out of college was in human resources, and I really enjoyed the work. That's when I fell in love with HR. I learned a lot of functions in HR: benefits, training, payroll and compensation, recruitment, employee relations, and I had exposure to the leadership team of the company. My colleague at the time decided to leave the company, and our manager was going to post for her replacement. I set up a meeting with my manager to let her know I was interested in taking on that role. That became my first promotion. I was proud that I asked for what I wanted. I was taught, as a Black woman, that hard work, perseverance, adaptability, and self-reliance are what you need to move ahead. As I continued my great work, I hoped to be promoted to supervisor, but was passed over. When I asked why, there was no reason given. I asked for feedback, as feedback is a gift on how to improve, and I was told I was doing the right things. So I decided to do the right thing for me and began looking for another opportunity somewhere else. Step out on faith and courage and ask for what you want or deserve and go after it; if you don't get what you want, keep trying and revise the plan.

I found my new place of work a couple of months later all while preparing to wed my high school sweetheart. I took the lessons I'd learned and my experiences to work at another company and moved up the ladder. This progress landed me at my third company.

I've enjoyed all the companies where I have worked. I have learned lessons and gained valuable experiences. Five years ago, here I go again, mustering up courage to ask for what I want; I asked to join the Diversity, Equity, and Inclusion (DEI) team. My work as a Human Resources Business Partner (HRBP) was very rewarding and fulfilling, but I was drawn to the work of DEI. I really enjoyed attending our cultural celebrations and building programs to help associates feel included and appreciated, and to feel a sense of belonging at work. I wanted—no, needed—to do work that was bigger than me. How and where could I make an impact on the lives of our associates? How could I make an impact on the culture of our organization and foster a philosophy of inclusion? It's an audacious goal, and a tenacious one.

Being part of the DEI team gave me a different kind of joy and sense of purpose. It was a small and mighty team, and this work of DEI takes true courage: courage to speak up and advocate for others; courage to show up as my true self and to help others do the same; courage to foster a work environment where everyone feels respected, seen, and heard; and courage to take criticism or face backlash with opposing perspectives. My work is nothing but tenacious, and my unwavering commitment to creating meaningful and positive change—long-term, positive change—takes time. I will take all the small incremental victories we get.

As I grew in my experience as a DEI practitioner, I and the team grew as well. We took the DEI work forward, and as soon as we were getting more traction, the pandemic hit and turned the world upside down. I never experienced so much anxiety, fear, and uncertainty in my life. I have always been a busy woman with my many commitments in and outside of work. The pandemic virus hit me hard, with lingering effects to this day, and this was a huge awaking for me. My husband said he had never seen me that sick in the thirty-six years we've known each other. It was a very scary time, and the virus literally sat me down and did a number on me.

But sitting still is what was needed, and with even more intention, I needed to listen to my friend and savior Jesus Christ. While I have always wanted to work in corporate America, I also wanted to own my own business. It was time to stop dreaming about being an entrepreneur and start taking the necessary steps to open my online jewelry business. My mom shared a letter that I wrote to myself when I was about sixteen years of age. The letter listed all the things I dreamed of achieving: I would graduate college, get married, and work in corporate America as an architect. Well, I did not become an architect of buildings, but I became an architect of my life. I have always been a planner who played it safe. This approach worked for me, but as I matured, I realized I was existing and not living. Don't get me wrong, life has been good, and I am proud of my accomplishments and connecting to the DEI work I am doing now; but there was this feeling of missing my purpose or missing my moment to be an entrepreneur.

In my conversation with God during this time of stillness, I birthed Made U Smile Jewelry. It's a handcrafted jewelry business where I design and construct all the pieces. This decision has been the best one I've ever made. Although it is scary at times, it gets me out of my comfort zone and pushes me in ways I did not know existed. Taking charge and leading hits differently when it's your baby. I like to think of my work and business as a living example of the way I express my tenacity, and here's some advice for you too:

Thick skinned—not everyone is going to like me or the work I perform or the jewelry I design, and that is OK because it's important to know your worth.

Encouraged and excited to continue my journey of what is yet to come and embrace what does come.

Notice what is working and not working and be alright with shifting goals to meet your vision.

Awareness to learn from my mistakes and the mistakes of others.

Courage to step in and out on faith to pursue goals and take risks.

I don't give up, but I may shift.

Timing—time is something we all want more of and don't have enough of, but it's not my timing; it's God's timing and being patient to know that when it is my time, I'll be ready and prepared.

Y—understanding my *why* drives my tenacity to stay the distance.

I've been blessed to have a wonderful corporate career and now my own business, and I'm grateful. There is a lot of life in me to do good work and make God proud. But in these moments of reflection, I think about the drive and persistence of my mother, and how she retired from one job and moved on to another, where she works today, and how in the face of adversity she keeps going. It's her smile that makes me proud, and for that I will never stop my tenacity. In the infamous words of DJ Khalid, "All I do is win, win, win no matter what."

Dawn Higgins has the satisfaction of serving as Director of Diversity, Equity, and Inclusion at Nestlé Purina and as founder and CEO of Made U Smile Jewelry LLC. She has the pleasure of fostering an inclusive work environment and the passion of handcrafting beautiful jewelry that radiates a smile.

Dawn earned a BA in Business Administration from Central Missouri State University and a MA in Human Resources Management from Webster University and holds two human resources certifications: Professional Human Resources and Society of Human Resource Management Certified Professional.

In the spirit of this scripture passage from the Gospel of Luke (12:48), "To whom is given, much is required," Dawn actively serves in leadership roles with community organizations and her sorority. She was recognized in 2023 as one of the "Top 100 St. Louisans to Know to Succeed in Business" by *Small Business Monthly* and is a Side Hustle Awardee.

Dawn enjoys spending time with her family and friends, especially her husband and silky terrier.

Shannon Grus

She Tried

Two little words that mean so much to me: She Tried. If you have known me for more than a hot minute and you give me a chance, you will understand how these two little words truly sum up my existence. Whether it is in relation to growing up, my marriage, my children, my career, my friends, my community, or quite frankly any wrong I see in the world, these are the two little words I would be proud to have engraved on my headstone.

Now some of you may ask, why "She tried" and not "She succeeded?" Well, quite simply, this is because being tenacious means I never stop trying.

Growing up in a small town, I was fortunate to have the very best parents one could ever ask for. They taught me love, kindness, respect, humility, and in many ways the most important trait: never give up on what and who you believe in.

In our home growing up, I shared my bedroom with my older sister. She is five years older, and when you are seven and she is twelve, that is a big age difference. We had very different views on how our room should be decorated. My side was filled with stuffed animals and Barbies, and on her side was a record player (yes—it was that long ago), perfume, and magazines. The actual décor of the room was our mom's decision, however, not ours. Our mom preferred a cozy look, so our room had two antique twin beds with matching quilts and afghan blankets made by our grandmothers.

On the wall on my side of the room, my mom hung a poem by Emily Dickinson. "If I Can Stop One Heart from Breaking" was scripted in a blue frame with blue gingham material matting and blue ricrac ribbon outlining the poem. It perfectly matched my bedroom with pale blue walls and a large dark-blue dresser (painted furniture was as in then as it is now). Little did I know that that quaintly framed poem would become my life's mantra.

The poem pushes the reader to not live in vain, to ease lives of aching and cool others' pains. It was powerful stuff to be in a young girl's bedroom. The verse that is the heart of the poem for me is: "If I can help one fainting robin unto his nest again, I shall not live in vain."

This verse and poem guide me in all I do in my life. There are "robins" all around us. I am driven to never give up and never stop trying to help them. This has been true over and over in my life. When I was nine years old, my mom asked me why there was a strange dog tied up in the backyard. Obviously, the dog had followed me home. and, not wanting him to get hit by a car as he tried to make his way back to his home, I tied him up. Then I called the vet with the rabies tag number (we did not have fancy chips back then) to get the owner's phone number to ask them to come and get the dog. Then there was the time my children's private school, with forty-two students from kindergarten age through eighth grade, needed new playground equipment. The school did not have the funds, so I started a dinner auction. After its inception and the seven subsequent years I chaired it, the event raised over six figures in donations, which provided not only the playground equipment but also new computers and capital improvements. The best part is that the dinner auction, founded through my tenacity, continues today!

The same framed poem, which so perfectly matched my childhood bedroom, is now hanging in my home. The frame is a mismatch to the updated décor, but I don't care. Though my life has taken many turns, I now reside with my husband in Rosebud, Missouri, and have for more than thirty years. After we had lived in our small town for about eight years, one day I was in the backyard hanging out with our dog—a small, overweight corgi mix, with blue eyes and no tail. A truck pulled up on the street behind our home, and a man got out and called, "Rebel!"—our dog's name. I suspect the man had some sort of food to entice our over-weight pet. The dog's name suited him; he never came when we called him. I immediately got up and yelled at Rebel, and the man drove off. I later found out that he was the town dog catcher, and he was paid by the dog. I also learned that if a dog was not picked up from the pound in three days, the dog was taken away and surrendered to a kill shelter. Welcome to another one of my tenacious moments! Within a week, I attended the Rosebud City Council meeting and voiced my concerns. My motivation? That poem, again. The verses inspire me to try, to become a person who will not stand by without getting involved in righting an injustice.

Helping robins is not about just talking; it is about doing. So flash forward from that city council meeting, and I have been Mayor of Rosebud for the past eighteen years. Speaking up is not enough. Fighting and trying for change is how to succeed.

The Emily Dickinson poem is so simple and yet so powerful. It speaks to me in an almost haunting way. But it is also my own superpower. I not only use this poem to motivate myself to keep trying but to encourage others to believe in their own ability to achieve success. You can do this in so many ways both large and small. I am that friend, colleague, or stranger you meet on the street who will encourage you to reach for your goal. I truly believe that each and every one of us is capable of doing anything we set our minds to. The only exception to this might be singing. My mom told me when I was a child it was best for me and those sitting around us if I just mouthed the songs in church. But even this is changing. Now there is autotune, and maybe everyone can be a singer—perhaps just not in church.

If you give people an opportunity, and provide them with support, it will change lives. This is why I work at State Technical College of Missouri. We provide students with transformational education, and we work to ensure that every one of them graduates and finds a fulfilling and successful career. I even have pom-poms in my office because I have been called the "Head Cheerleader" at State Tech! I believe in higher education so much that I permanently endowed a scholarship. This is my way of believing and providing support for a stranger who has the desire to change his or her life. What better way to lift a robin?

The poem directs us to lift robins. It quite literally tells us to keep trying. Your robin might be always putting money in the Salvation Army kettle, it might be offering a friendly smile to a stranger, or it might be pushing your company to the next level, knowing it is the right thing for everyone.

When I say, "She tried," I mean "Try to be tenacious in your life." Live knowing that without starting there is no finish, but without trying there is no success. Try to be tenacious in doing the right thing, and try to be tenaciously grateful for opportunities given to you. Try to be tenaciously supportive of others and help lift them up to allow them to succeed. Most importantly, be tenacious in trying to be the very best version of yourself every day—use autotune if needed. Be proud if, at the end of the day, someone says, "She tried."

Shannon Grus is a master of trying to make the world a better place. She is a serial doer, who over the years has committed to many nonprofit and community projects due to her inability to say "no" to a great idea or cause.

She is currently Vice President of External Relations at State Technical College of Missouri, as well as Mayor of Rosebud. However, Shannon's greatest achievements are her family, including her incredibly supportive husband, Steve; her daughter, Sophie, and Sophie's fiancé, Mark; and her son, Samuel.

She loves living in small-town America and walking daily with her dogs Cecelia and Penny. When not at work, walking her dogs, or performing mayor duties, you will find Shannon relaxing at the Lake of the Ozarks with friends and family.

Kimberly Liebert

Honing Your Tenacity

Tenacity is a word that embodies a sense of being. It can be a sense of purpose in a specific situation; it can be a guiding principle in one's life; it can be an emotional state, or all these combined. It is something you can possess and carry with you, as if this sense of resolve was in your biological makeup. However, it does not come naturally for most, and you can learn tenacity as a skill. This skill will set you apart on both a professional and personal level.

Let's first understand tenacity and its importance, and then look at key steps to building this skill.

What is Tenacity? According to Oxford Languages, the definition of tenacity is:

- the quality or fact of being very determined; determination.
- the quality or fact of continuing to exist, persistence.
- **Tenacity is similar to** persistence, determination, perseverance, strength of will, and relentlessness.
- **Its opposite is** irresolution or lack of resolve.

What is Tenacity in Leadership?

According to *Forbes*, tenacity is "a fierce blend of determination, persistence, and grit." For leaders and their organizations, it is an attribute that can mean the difference between failure and success and can move a team from "doing all right" to "thriving."

Why Is Tenacity Important for Success?

Studies show that tenacity is one of the most critical attributes of achievement. Having perseverance and passion for long-term goals is essential. Studies have shown that **grit was a stronger prediction of high achievement than IQ**. *Success is often not a matter of talent, but a matter of tenacity – Nathaniel Bronner*

Examples of Tenacity

- Oprah Winfrey faced enormous adversity in both her professional and personal lives. The talk show host and businesswoman was publicly fired from her first job as a TV anchor in Baltimore because she was "too emotionally invested in her stories." Winfrey went onto create a media empire and became one of the most acclaimed experts in television. She's worth an estimated cool $2.4 billion, according to *Forbes*.

- Sheryl Sandberg, known for her activism and as Facebook's COO, has overcome her share of adversity. According to *Time* Magazine, she fought her way to the top of her industry (whilst promoting women in business along the way), then sadly lost her husband unexpectedly in 2015. In true Sandberg style, the author wrote about his death in her second book, *Option B: Facing Adversity, Building Resilience, and Finding Joy*, which offered guidance on overcoming hardship.

- At Harvard, Ruth Bader Ginsburg learned to balance life as a mother and her new role as a law student. Biography.com recounts her story of pursuing her degree in a very male-dominated, hostile environment, with only eight females in her class of five hundred. The women were chided by the law school's dean for taking the places of qualified males. But Ginsburg pressed on and excelled academically, eventually becoming a member of the prestigious legal journal, the *Harvard Law Review*. Despite her outstanding academic record, Ginsburg continued to encounter gender discrimination while seeking employment after graduation. Ruth went on to serve twenty-seven years as a justice on the Supreme Court.

Is Tenacity a Skill?

Stubbornness means clinging to what you know, while being tenacious is about steadily moving forward. **Tenacity is a great skill** and a way of being that you can develop in your life. Tenacious people **don't rely on luck, fate, or destiny for their success.** When conditions become difficult, they keep working. They know that trying times are no time to quit trying. That's what makes the difference.

The single difference between successful people with this skill is the ability to *act*. And keep in mind, the ability to understand when to quit is also an important skill.

The most difficult thing is the decision to act, the rest is merely tenacity.

– *Amelia Earhart*

Ten Steps to Build the Skill of Tenacity:

1. **Develop a vision for what you want.** Set a clear long-term vision for what you want to achieve and then set goals surrounding that vision, similar to milestones in a project with subtasks to achieve each milestone.

2. **Set clear goals.** Write down your goals on an annual basis or whatever frequency is meaningful to you. Create them in time components that are manageable and can be achieved in that time frame. Writing goals down makes them more tangible and holds you accountable.

3. **Manage your thinking.** Keep your eye on the prize with self-talk and focus. Do not let outside factors influence your focus or let self-defeat seep into your mindset. Self-talk can be a powerful tool to provide frequent reminders of your longer-term goals and help you rise above momentary setbacks.

4. **Put in preparation.** The key to being a tenacious person is going above and beyond when it comes to preparation. "Practice makes perfect" applies here. Keeping a task list, setting reminders, and rehearsing your talking points all are keys to being prepared. You need to even be overprepared. In my experience, this comes easier when you are passionate about your vision and goals, and they become almost second nature in your speech and interactions.

5. **Learn from mistakes, both yours and others.** No one will ever be perfect, and you will experience highs and lows along your journey. But taking in learning from your mistakes or situations or observing others' same struggles will help you pivot to refining your vision and goals and becoming better as a result.

6. **Find the benefits in adversity.** We will all face adversity along the way. This can be the hardest step for most of us as we need to take a bad situation and see the benefit or opportunity that bloomed from it. It may also take time to see these benefits and opportunities to allow for the "sting" to wear off and embrace healing from the adversity first to transition to see the benefits. I believe in the adage that you may not understand at the time why something happened to you, but when you get beyond it and find success later, in hindsight you will see the journey led to your ultimate success.

7. **Be forward-looking and seek opportunities.** Do not let opportunities pass you by. You may not be ready, but look forward to any opportunities no matter how big or small and seize the moment. Take the first six steps to get ready yourself. It may never be the perfect time, but you will be ready enough to grasp the moment.

8. **Know your worth.** Walk with confidence in all that you do. You know your worth, and this needs to come across to everyone else. You know hard you have worked and what you have to offer. Instill this truth in your mindset and know who you are and that you can accomplish what you've envisioned.

9. **Never allow the fear of failing to control you.** This step immobilizes many. Fear takes over the will to succeed and results in not trying

at all. The difference between those who are successful and those who are not is the power to "act." Someone else may have more skills or pedigree, but a person's willingness to pursue their goal and to try sets them apart. If you never try, you will never know, and you will certainly never realize your vision.

10. **Never give up on your dreams.** All of us have successes and failures. If you let failures or momentary setbacks dictate your vision, you will never realize your dream. Keep going. Use the first nine steps to help you achieve Step 10. Get back on the proverbial horse, ride again, and ride into the sunset of your success. Tenacity is the power to never give up on yourself.

Do not let other people or circumstances dictate your goals.

You will have supporters and those who want to undermine your success. At times certain people feel threatened by the pursuit of your goals, and you will need to rise above this. Keep in mind that they may have remained immobilized to "act," and you have not. You keep going, and that is the difference for you and your success. Tenacity will set you forward.

There is a "self-talk" quote I use to keep moving forward. It empowers me especially in times of difficulty. Find your own quote to use and keep telling yourself, willing yourself to succeed. *But still, like air, I rise - Maya Angelou*

Tenacity can be learned as a skill and is critical to success. The best part about tenacity is that it is an equal skill for all. It does not cost a dime, and anyone can learn it. It does not require a high level of intelligence, an Ivy League education, or your exposure to certain social circles. It is completely free and up to you to employ, and it will be the skill that sets you apart from the rest.

Kimberly Liebert is the founder, president, and CEO of Leigh Consulting. Leigh Consulting is a world-class technology and consulting firm with core competencies in technology and management services.

Kimberly is a dynamic and proven leader with more than twenty-five years of technology management experience and is a certified CPA. With a balance of business expertise, extensive technology knowledge, and project management experience, Kimberly is a true asset to her clients. Proven project delivery and alignment of strategy has achieved strong, long-term relationships with Leigh Consulting clients.

Kimberly is responsible for developing relationships and fostering client engagement as well as leading the Leigh Consulting team.

Cindy Mebruer

Tenacious-Level Thinking & the 59 Ways to Get There

"Well-behaved women seldom make history."

- Laurel Thatcher Ulrich

You have probably not met Cindy Mebruer. If you know her, then you're aware she's not at all comfortable writing a chapter about herself. But she's going to do it for three reasons. They go something like this...

First, she's always wanted to be a writer (unless she could be president of the United States or a hockey goalie. She also invented Airbnb's when she was six years old; we'll circle back to this!). She began her master's work at Washington University–St. Louis (WUSTL) in Comparative Literature. She garnered high marks and praise for her essays, research, and was spotlighted to speak on her creative writing piece. About midway through this endeavor, however, she wondered what in the world she would do with this degree. Becoming a sandal-wearing, tunic-draped sage is everyone's dream, right? Just not sure anyone would pay for such an ethereal endeavor. Also during this time, Cindy was a single mom of three. One year she and all three of her kids were in college at the same time! It was hectic, energizing, and so much fun for this tight family of four; she's still got the student loans to prove it! Thus, the role of a penniless Socrates was off the table. But the question "what to do" lingered.

For the majority of Cindy's career, a job change was preceded by someone asking her to join their organization. These opportunities were and are, incredible chapters of her professional life; it's an honor to know folks believe she's the right person at that right time. But on a particularly elder-number birthday, she began to wonder about her choices. Cindy has vast and unique industry experiences: cosmetology to commercial/residential real estate; special education to supply chain. Though Cindy knows how to be a Jackie-of-all-trades, a nagging question continues: what does Cindy want to do? Thus, the second reason she's jumping on board the GRIT ship: she's thinking this exercise in self-awareness mixed with a dash of self-honesty will help find the answers. Though, before we continue, let's give thanks.

Our anthology authors and GRIT comrades know, no one can say no to Jennifer Bardot. (Unintentional rhyming…see, the study of Comparative Literature comes in handy). Though Cindy's not at Jennifer's level of networking prowess, she's not far off. One of Jennifer's many strengths is she has a knack for creating opportunities for those around her to shine. It's her superpower. Cindy has flavors of this; Cindy's strength is to see your strength: see the purpose of your mission, help you bring your product or service into the light of the market, and connect you with the people who can make you and your business shine. At present, Cindy is helping her team foster their growth, helping colleagues and friends find the right connections, and spreading the gospel of the CSCMP's (see bio) new initiatives, housed in our Center for the Advancement of Talent & Training. (Commercial break: for more information on how we will use our training tools to help populations overlooked but with untapped potential get good jobs with good companies, please reach out!)

Truth be told, and side-lining the third-person script, I am both an introvert and an extrovert; both can be true at the same time. As I love big music festivals, SC City soccer games, CSCMP's Global Edge Conference, and hosting all of our family gatherings, my recharge routine is far more simple: a good book and a great bottle of wine outside by a fire!

Please do not mistake my laborious and droll third-person humor above as an attempt at false bravado or some sort of self-acknowledgement, I am hilarious. I'm hiding in plain sight, attempting in vain to obfuscate my little "impostor syndrome" voice. Most times, I can keep this whisperer at bay. But this assignment is me saying yes to things I know will make me sweat, and, more so, recognizing, honoring, and putting to good use my own superpowers. Thus, this chapter, book, and opportunity is me leaping out of my quite comfortable, comfort zone!

I'm rewriting what I believe is my fifty-ninth draft of this essay; this is only a partially sarcastic assessment. This also happens to be my fifty-ninth birthday. That's right, fifty-nine! I've got the husband, three kids, two step kids, two sons-in-laws, one daughter-in-law, two granddaughters, two grandsons, and one step grandson to go along with this big, bold number...and I wouldn't have it any other way! Getting weirded out by age has never been my thing. I look at this (really big) number as a blessing. You get to what folks call "a certain age" and you can grumble a little bit, telling stories about how you walked uphill, no shoes, in the snow, to school every day. But that's not me and it certainly isn't the women in our family either. My grandma, who was our tenacious matriarch, brandished her strengths and intellect with quiet wit (the kind of statements you don't get until later on). Sayings like, "If you don't eat, it's your own fault" or "Nothing good happens after midnight unless you're home with those you love." We'd roll our eyes, but turns out she was right. Thus, with age comes...

You thought I was going to say wisdom, didn't you? Well, there is that. But there's more; with age comes—say it with me—tenacity! As you get older, your armor is stronger, your ideas are bolder, and you become formidably fearless! This tenacity fuels us with the courage to tackle new challenges and the strength to crush them. Which brings me to my third point, though not before tidying up loose ends.

I cannot be a hockey goalie because I cannot skate. And because I ran for a Board of Alder position three times and lost, I don't suspect I'll get to be US president anytime soon. (I campaign horribly for myself, but it turns out I'm quite successful getting others elected; thus the mayor I helped win appointed me for the post I lost when the guy who won had to leave town. Take that, guy who won the election!) The good news is as long as I turn in this essay, I will officially be a published writer, alongside the amazing, incredible, and learned GRIT women I admire so much! Because of our collective move toward tenacious living, I want to challenge myself even more. So here goes . . .

Remember earlier when I made the bold assertion I invented the idea of Airbnb's? Cleary this is an untrue statement, but when we were living with my grandma, I built a five-star hotel and very fancy restaurant, in her home. She had an unfinished basement full of antique furniture, lots of play fabric, dusty picture frames, shelves of old books, and old telephones (my grandfather worked for Ma Bell). It was a make-believe dream space! She knew I was "building a business," so she would bring home her partially used accounting binders from the bowling alley where she worked, and let me use her old typewriter (now vintage and on my bookshelf). Though we never left the basement, the geography of our establishment changed constantly. We were located in the mountains one day, nestled on a beach the next. I was the owner, operator, head chef, and, most importantly, President of Everything. Everyone was welcome, though only girls were allowed to work there. The name of this incredible suite of desirable destination spots: The Ladies Landing. Stay with me.

I recently listened to the podcast *Something Extra*, hosted by GRIT author Lisa Nichols, in which she interviewed Dana Spinola. Of the many fantastic nuggets Dana shared about opening her store Fab'rik, what caught my attention was when she was building her business, she did so on two fronts: she created a space within an industry she loves, which would fill her with joy, and she created an opportunity to help those in situations which break her heart. She found ways to bring joy, purpose, and support to those who have been trafficked. The latter is something I have been thinking about since 2014, when I presented my MLA paper on sex trafficking. I shared theories on how to break this underground supply chain and offered approaches toward helping those who have been rescued find their way back to their lives. Within the next two to five years, I would like to build a business which in part, employs women who have been trafficked and/or justice-impacted. I'll partner with organizations to help provide pathways toward work/life integration via training and long-term support services. It's not exactly the Ladies Landing, but I do believe the time I spent "running" my business has turned out to be the "industry experience" that has stayed with me!

I am sharing this with you not to solicit partners; it's to challenge myself to do this. I've been mulling this idea over and over in my head for years. Many of you have an idea growing in your heads and hearts, I'll bet. Seems it's time, my Tenacious Friends, for all of us to put pencil to paper, make our plans, and build our dreams! This is me stepping out of my comfort zone, utilizing my strengths to chart my own path toward a destination I will create. I invite you to join me. Looks like 59 is the Year of the Tenacious. So ladies, let's go make some history!

Cindy Mebruer is Director of Education, Engagement & Sustainability for the Talent Center of Excellence (TCE), within the Council of Supply Chain Management Professionals (CSCMP). She has spent her professional career within a supply chain/academic setting, focusing on professional/student development, customized training, executive education, optimization consulting in SCM/Operations/Leadership, and event/conference execution. At present, Cindy builds and executes the Training to Jobs Initiative (T2J). The T2J program promotes the future of supply chain employment by providing customized training to those who have been underserved, underutilized, and overlooked while meeting the employment needs of partner companies.

Cindy was a member of the second Civilian Commanders cohort at Scott Air Force Base, 2018–2020. A member of the board of directors for Boone Center, Inc., she serves as Vice Chair of the executive committee as well as Chair Emeritus and Member of the development committee. She is a mentor within the St. Louis IT Leadership Development Program, a member of the YMCA Regional Association Board of Directors, and she cofounded the St. Louis Operations Collective, which hosts the Convergence Industry Conference each year.

Mary Enderle

The White Boots

Some stories can only be told simply, without dialogue or drama. My story is one of those. And for anyone who might have warned me that I would become an empty nester and a widow within two months, I would have said you were absolutely crazy, but that is exactly what happened to me in 2022.

Brian, my husband, and I had been married since June 2001. Brian served our country from 1994 to 1998 in the Marine Corps, which was a major influence in his life. I was a single mother to my six-year-old daughter and just starting my career in transportation when we were married. Then we bought our home and our son was born.

In 2021, I was getting restless, feeling creative and ready to take on a challenge. I asked Brian what he thought about starting an online business as a side hustle. I was thinking along the lines of a boutique for dog apparel. Brian always wanted to make T-shirts, so we decided to do both.

Part of our inspiration came from a desire to help veterans suffering from PTSD. We named our company Devil Dog Worx and began networking so we could give back to local veteran organizations. The timing was good, as our daughter had just moved to Maine to become a morning news anchor, leaving her room empty. We had our workshop and our mission, and off we went.

We marketed our products at various car shows and country music festivals. I interacted with the public, and Brian managed behind the scenes. At Freedom Jam, a country music festival, we were introduced to the Forgotten Coast K9 Organization. We decided to make them one of the beneficiaries of our merchandise sales.

About that time, our son made his choice of career paths. He wanted to become a Marine and follow in his dad's footsteps. At one of our pop-up events, we met a local Marine Corps recruiter who started talking to our son, who mentioned that he had an appointment at the recruiting office that following Monday. That conversation filled me with apprehension, as it confirmed we would not be leaving that office without signing documents and starting the enlistment process. Everything was changing so suddenly. I was glad I had the business to focus on.

With the country music festival just around the corner, I started incorporating beautiful rhinestone fringe jean jackets into the Devil Dog Worx merchandise. I'd had a lot of experience over the years adding stones to my daughter's competition dance costumes, so I added these jackets to the website. The process of creating something so beautiful helped me focus. They were a terrific item to start promoting and helped keep my mind off the fact that our son would soon be leaving for boot camp to become a marine.

My birthday was coming up, and Brian asked me what I wanted. He always gave over-the-top gifts for birthdays and Christmas, and he even wrapped the presents with each person's special wrapping paper. I'd seen these beautiful, white, country western boots and knew that's what I wanted. When he asked me, I gave him that silly "Oh you don't have to give me anything" response, knowing we were on a budget. I did mention the boots to him, though.

What Brian didn't know was that he would also be getting a gift. I'd received a phone call in mid-August from the country western concert organizer stating that the Forgotten Coast K9 Organization would be presenting two service dogs to two veterans at the event. They had chosen Brian, and the presentation would be held onstage. They wanted the whole thing to be a surprise and use it to build community support. The concert organizer told me that all of the participating organizations had agreed that Brian should be one of the recipients. I promised that I wouldn't say a word to him.

Our son had enlisted with three other young men from our area. I called them the Fab 4. On September 3rd, we hosted a send-off party. A lot of people were there to help celebrate.

On September 6th, my husband woke up with severe stomach pains and was throwing up. I wondered if he'd picked up a virus being around all the people who had shown up at the party. I also thought that of all the times to be sick, this was the worst. The Forgotten Coast K9 Organization was presenting the service dog to Brian on Saturday. I hoped it would pass quickly so he would be able to be onstage for the presentation. That turned out to not be the case. Brian was feeling worse as the week went on. On the day of the country music festival, I hoped he could show up just for thirty minutes, but he was too sick to attend. The organizers asked if I would accept the honors.

To be honest, I was upset with him. I definitely did not feel right receiving that award onstage; I am not a veteran, and he was the one who fought for our country. He deserved such recognition. Here I was, going up on that stage wearing my rhinestone fringe jacket and my new beautiful white country western boots that Brian had surprised me with earlier. He wanted me to make sure I had them for my birthday.

I was so excited when I got home that evening, eager to tell Brian about the presentation, and the thirty-week training program they awarded him along with a service dog. He was already asleep when I got home, so I had to wait until the next day to tell him. That same day we took our son to the hotel where he would stay until being flown to boot camp. I didn't like knowing we wouldn't have any contact with him for thirteen weeks. I took so many pictures of my husband and son together. We had no idea that father-son goodbye hug would be their last.

Our son flew to San Diego on September 12th, and on September 13th Brian was worse. He was dehydrated and had severe stomach pains. We went to the emergency room and waited nearly three hours for the tests to come back. When the doctor finally came into the room with the results, I saw the look on her face and knew it wasn't going to be good. She told us that Brian was jaundiced. He needed a stint in his bile duct because he was nearly septic from the bile that was spilling over into his system. And that he would need emergency surgery because they found a mass on his pancreas.

Talk about having your world flipped upside down. It was a double punch to the gut. My mind started racing. Everything changed in an instant. I couldn't focus. All of these questions, what do we do, what is next, what happens if it is cancer, how do I make these stomach pains go away from my husband who is lying in the bed? How do I tell my family, my children? I had no way of calling our son because he was in boot camp.

Then I thought, "This is part of Brian's testimony. That's it! This is part of his story because he is going fight this and be that miracle. He will be telling his story to friends and strangers while we are on the road as empty nesters. He will have his service dog. He will help veterans and first responders get their service dogs." Such thoughts gave me strength and hope. Until we found out he had Stage 4 pancreatic cancer and the cancer had spread.

Tenacity is a word I don't often use, and yet tenacity exemplified everything that happened next. Even when everything fell apart, I had to be resolute. I had to hold it together for my children. I reached out to Brian's primary physician, who helped us get through everything. I called the Red Cross to be put in touch with our son. Our daughter flew home when Brian was starting chemo in mid-October. Shortly thereafter, he took a drastic turn for the worse. He was placed on hospice November 3rd. He lost his battle on November 4th, 2022.

Writing this feels unreal. I am so thankful for the tremendous support our community, family, and friends provided when we were all completely shattered. I will always remember the elegance and precision of his funeral with full military honors, and the echo of the taps.

Survival can come down to just being able to sleep at night, which I am again. I have Sophie, our beautiful service dog, who brings me peace. She is an extension of Brian. I remind myself that my mission is to carry on my husband's legacy to help veterans. Last but not least, I know my journey is to find out who "Mary" is. I know that, with Sophie by my side, I will take each step, bravely wearing a fringe jacket studded with jewels and my white country western boots.

Mary Enderle began her career in transportation and logistics twenty years ago, holding various positions in business development. She was married to her husband Brian for twenty-one years, losing him to Stage 4 pancreatic cancer in November 2022. Mary has a twenty-eight-year-old daughter who is a morning news anchor, and a nineteen-year-old son currently serving in the United States Marine Corps. In addition to her full-time career, she and her late husband started an e-commerce business called Devil Dog Worx Apparel, specializing in T-shirts, dog bandanas, and rhinestone fringe jean jackets. They promoted them at various pop-up car shows and country music festivals to support veterans, many of whom suffer in silence from food instability, loneliness, isolation, and homelessness. Devil Dog Worx Apparel gives back to charitable organizations that provide support to veterans, including the Forgotten Coast K9 Organization, which honored her husband and presented him with a service dog just before he passed in 2022. Mary speaks on several podcasts and carries on Brian's legacy by sharing the mission of the Forgotten Coast K9 Organization.

Kathy Kilo Peterson

Can't Means Won't

Agreeing to write this chapter took me out of my comfort bubble. But I've learned that expanding your bubble of comfort is essential to growth. By expanding comfort, the uncomfortable becomes familiar. I'd like you to learn from my story about dealing with adversity, minimizing the devastating effects of stress, and knowing the enormous strength that lies dormant within us all. Adversity tests us. As we climb out of the valley of hurt, grief, or despair, we reach the summit only to see more mountains to climb on the horizon. As Ralph Waldo Emerson said, "Life is a journey, not a destination." The dangers of these adversities are that stress can cause enormous damage to our body. The damage that stress hormones create is expressed as disease. Ask me how I know.

Tenacity has a component of fierceness and vulnerability. This may seem like an odd combination, but when faced with adversity, it takes vulnerability to not only ask for help but to accept it and succumb to it. The vulnerability piece multiplies the fierceness. When I face a challenge, I take some moments of intentional breathing and even short meditation. Then the fierceness is unleashed, but in a controlled and methodical manner to tackle the challenge. I've adopted this method as the result of much inner work and with the help of many. The goal is to overcome obstacles without the harmful impact of long-term stress and unresolved trauma. We will never live a life free from adversity and challenges, and who would want to, anyway? Without any challenges, life would be stagnant and void of personal growth.

In sharing my experiences, I decided to provide only a few snippets so that the story doesn't sound like the lyrics for the next country song. I'm a very positive energy person, so I do not like to dwell in drama. My story began about twenty-four years ago. Within the span of a few years, via deceit, my seven-figure net worth vaporized into a negative sum. Upon confronting him, I was strangled by my (former) husband, and my two-year-old daughter, Lucy, and I were held hostage in our home.

After this happened, my dad said some comforting words. He reminded me that my former husband only took the one thing that could be replaced: money. He did not take Lucy, and he did not take my smile. The next years were filled with a constant barrage of evil and disruption.

Fast-forward to 2020, when my beautiful, silly, smart daughter was abducted. It's been three and one-half years since she's been gone, and life is very different. The hardest part to overcome was the guilt of failing at a parent's top responsibility: to protect your child. I felt like I had failed miserably. How had I not seen the deeper signs? This was the start of a very long and enduring inner struggle for me. In those early years, my Number One Goal was to protect my child. I focused on two things: Lucy and my business. I now see that I should have added a third focus: me.

I'm grateful to have always had an amazing, supportive team in my business. I have been a servant leader throughout my career, and it has served me and my team well. During those years, I was "all in" when I was at work. When I was at home, I was all in. Even through those years of constant attack, my State Farm office has been one of the top in the country. Where I failed was taking care of myself. I thought I was doing all the right things. By not letting the threats control my life, I had my "turtle shell" on. I was determined that his actions would not alter my way of living. Yes, I was hyper aware of my surroundings, but I refused to live in fear. I shielded all emotion (other than positivity) from my daughter, and I compartmentalized the fear and stress into a little box to avoid its disruption in our lives.

Little did I know the damaging effects of that stress. Living in stress is like stepping on the gas and the brake at the same time. Nothing good happens in that scenario, especially over a long period of time. The body breaks down. The immune system is compromised. This is where my next journey started. This is when synchronicities came to life. Once you are faced with your own mortality, the mind shifts. This is when fierceness and vulnerability embraced for me.

One day at the office in May 2007, I discovered I was unable to place my hand flat on my desk. "Darn it, I'm getting arthritis," I told myself. Pain and swelling in my hands and arms soon followed. During my first visit to the Center for Advanced Medicine, seven medical students appeared in my exam room. They were brought in to witness someone with a rare disease that brought with it a prognosis that 50 percent of patients live up to five years. Systemic scleroderma was the diagnosis. They call it the "turn to stone" disease. The online photos were not pretty. My lung function had plummeted to 50 percent. The students, in their fresh white lab coats, entered my room with crossed arms and concerned faces. I immediately said, "Whoa! Lighten up—it's going to be OK!" I knew I would heal because I had Lucy to protect and to finish teaching her all the life skills she would need.

Rumi said, "Where there is a wound, light shall enter it."

When our minds are open, people are put in our path at the exact moment we need them. My incredible rheumatologist, who by coincidence had trained under the godfather of scleroderma at Johns Hopkins, scheduled me for occupational therapy (along with a slew of other things). At my first OT session, the therapist I was supposed to see was sick, so I saw an excellent young therapist who shared the name of a person who performs some "nontraditional" therapy. Her background was physical therapy, applied with mystical, healing hands.

A few weeks after my diagnosis, a friend invited me, at the last minute, to join a group of friends for the Cardinals baseball game; they had an extra ticket. I decided to go and sat next to a woman I had not met before. She was brave enough to ask what happened to my hands, and she shared her personal experience with a Chinese medicine doctor trained at Washington University School of Medicine. The doctor had given up his Western medicine practice and switched to Chinese medicine after his own experiences and research. She offered to personally take me to see him. The synchronicities continued. My team gave me the most special gift: a prayer bracelet, called a "Praycelet." They had each taken turns wearing the bracelet while praying for my health and for Lucy, then they gave it to me. I wore it every day until a few years later when I was on a field trip with Lucy to Cahokia Mounds. I lost the bracelet that day, and if I had to lose it, that was the perfect place. The ancient Cahokia Mounds served as a central religious pilgrimage city. I am also a Taurus and feel a special connection to Mother Earth.

These coincidences and synchronicities were each vital to my healing. Opening to vulnerability and to possibility allowed the pieces to intersect with my path. Throughout this journey, I have lived in gratitude for each experience, each connection, and for all that I have. So many people focus on the "don't haves" and "if only's" and live in the past. If you live in the past over the present, then you are not creating your own reality. You are choosing to relive the past in the present day. That is not where growth occurs. Suffering is experienced by all. Healing and transformation are experienced by few. Dorcy Pruter said, "It's hard until it isn't." Of course, then it gets hard again…until it isn't. Our health, both mentally and physically, reflects how we have or have not worked through life's challenges, traumas, and struggles. If we learn to understand and work through the trauma points—micro and macro—we heal ourselves. A program that helps me immensely is Higher Purpose Mastery. It opened my eyes to the why and how. Early childhood experiences and traumas, even micro traumas, all have an impact on all the choices we've made in life. As Dorcy Pruter says, "You must do the work." It's hard, really hard, and incredibly rewarding.

Now each day begins with gratitude, meditation, and a good workout before leaving for the office. My lung function is 100 percent, my business is thriving, and my friendships have deepened. Every day is one day closer to reuniting with Lucy. My goal is to be as strong mentally, spiritually, and physically as possible so that, once we are reunited, Lucy will have the strongest support possible for her healing. I have forgiven him. I did it for me, not for him. I have released him from me. He is no longer my battle.

I am confident that I gave Lucy a strong foundation to call upon in her own life's challenges: kindness (above all), hard work, silliness, respect, a love of nature, and a wonderment of living things. The four-letter word that was not allowed in our house was "can't." It was not allowed because "can't" means "won't." This motto and these core strengths are what will carry Lucy to the ultimate freedom she deserves: the freedom to be her authentic self, free from her captors and free from the conditions placed upon her. I know deep in my heart and in my soul that she will have the strength to be free soon. We will reunite. We are Tenacious.

Kathy Kilo Peterson is an inventor and entrepreneur. She has a design patent and a utility patent. She has owned her State Farm Insurance Agency for twenty-three years. Kathy has one daughter, Lucy, and a pup named Vinnie who is the official mascot and greeter in her office. Kathy is very involved in the community and in wildlife conservation. She takes pride in enhancing the forest at her farm outside Wildwood, Missouri, with a focus on increasing native habitat.

Kathy and her team have led her State Farm Agency to be one of the top agencies in the country. They've achieved President's Club status for three years, which represents the top fifty out of twenty thousand agents, and they've earned Chairmen's Circle for thirteen years, representing the top tier agencies in the country. Kathy was a "40 Under 40" award recipient of the *St. Louis Business Journal* in 2006.

Kathy believes communication and relational integrity are the pillars of success.

Kelli Risse

Breaking Through the Mess of Stress

Tenacity is in my DNA. I made the decision to walk away from a lucrative career—leaving behind financial security, seniority, and a name for myself—and step into entrepreneurship. It was a risk I was willing to take. After all, I've been taking risks my entire life—competing in pageants, auditioning for leads in musicals, and moving across the country alone. My determination to become an entrepreneur was fueled by a desire to impact others' lives at a deeper level while living a happy and fulfilled life. I've learned being a business owner comes with remarkable rewards and unexpected circumstances and that how you handle these determines your peace, joy, and happiness.

As a high achiever, it is always my goal to do my best and be my best, which means continually pushing myself out of my comfort zone. They say living outside your comfort zone is where personal growth happens. Based on my experiences, I believe that to be true. Living outside your comfort zone takes tenacity—courage, determination, and the ability to keep doing something difficult—and faith.

In the past decade, two areas of my life have required me to dig deep, draw upon my tenacious nature, and address my flawed thinking in order to live my best life and pursue my dreams. In 2017, the same year I started my coaching and speaking business, Rise Up and Live Wellness, I also found out my body was in a state of adrenal fatigue.

From 2010 to 2017, my stress personalities, as I like to refer to them in my signature talk "Breaking Through The Mess of Stress," reared their ugly heads. You might be wondering, "What's a 'stress personality'? Do I have them too?" Based on my extensive research and personal experiences, I am confident stress is a mind game and we all have stress personalities. We each create our own stress by *who* we are being and how we respond to situations that have meaning for us. We stress about what we care about.

Based on neuroscience, our subconscious programs create the stress we experience. The way we internalized our childhood experiences (upbringing, culture, education, media, entertainment, and peer influence) created our most fundamental beliefs, thoughts, and emotional patterns. For this reason, every human brings a unique perspective to a situation. Depending on their subconscious programs, two individuals may perceive the same experience as pleasant, positive, and uplifting, or as negative, degrading, and stressful.

My stress was created by the high expectations and pressure I put on myself to succeed, as well as my perfectionism, both directly related to the many years I spent in the performing arts. I was impatient, a trait I learned from my dad. I thought I could do it all, thanks to new societal norms, and overextended myself in all areas of my life. As if that wasn't enough, I would also worry. As a child I watched my grandma worry about everything. I worried about my kids, being number one in my career, and if I was doing life "right." My stress personalities—high achiever, perfectionist, superwoman, impatient, rule follower—resulted in burnout, exhaustion, and adrenal fatigue. My body was in a constant state of fight or flight, intensified by high-impact workouts, caffeine, and lack of sleep.

As an impatient high-achiever, I accepted the challenge of healing my body like I had accepted most challenges in my life—game on! What I didn't realize was my distorted thinking was preventing me from healing. *High Achiever Me* believed taking it easy or relaxing meant I was lazy. *Perfectionist Me* believed I had to be perfect to show my worth. *Rule Follower Me* believed there was a right way and wrong way to live, not an array of possibilities depending on the situation and person. *Impatient Me* believed everyone should be in a hurry and life should move fast. *Superwoman Me* believed I could do it all, handle it all, and be everything to everyone. Talk about exhausting! No wonder I was on the verge of burnout and my body and mind were fatigued. In hindsight, my body was giving me signs, clues, and warnings to change the way I was thinking and living.

To heal my body, I had to get out of "fight or flight" and into "rest and digest." That meant trading my adrenaline rush of high-intensity workouts for walking and yoga. Talk about a mindset shift. Remember "all or nothing"? I firmly believed if I was going to spend time working out, it better be at 110 percent so I could burn the most calories possible. You know what doesn't burn an immense number of calories or provide an avenue to take out your stress and aggressions? Walking and yoga! However, I am proud to say that with a lot of inner work, reflection, and tenacity to move through the uncomfortableness of going against my high-intensity beliefs, my body was able to heal. Are there days when I revert to high intensity? You bet! Then I remind myself to look at the long game—having a healthy body for many years to come.

As a business owner, I find myself constantly addressing my stress personalities and, more importantly, the thoughts that keep me stuck and running on the hamster wheel. This can be anything from chasing shiny new objects (aka more business tools), comparing myself to others, doing things I could delegate, or trying to control things completely out of my control.

My guess is you can probably relate even if you're not a business owner. How many times have you tried to control what other people think of you? How often do you waste time on the noise from social media, positive or negative, preventing you from building or staying consistent with a new habit?

In 2020, two and a half years into being a business owner, the pandemic brought unparalleled uncertainty to the business world. In my lifetime, there has never been a more stressful world-wide situation. Nonessential workers were forced to work from home, kids were sent home to learn virtually, and toilet paper was in great demand. Stress was at an all-time high as we navigated the uncertainty of what was supposed to last for two weeks. Supplies were limited, restaurants closed, and companies went out of business. I, too, had to decide what to do about my business.

Tenacity kept me from quitting my business. I chose to focus on what I could control, which were my personal habits of morning prayer, meditation, journaling, exercising, and putting on "real" clothes. I engaged in conversations with other business owners who knew that one's mindset was of the utmost importance. I thought the fact that I help business owners, entrepreneurs, and high-performing professionals reduce stress would play out well for my business. As it turned out, most women were too stressed to address their stress. It's like they were drowning and couldn't see above water to get help…a feeling I knew all too well. I decided the best thing to do was to be a resource in the community. Two nights a week I offered free virtual Fireside Chats for women who needed accountability and a support system. I was determined to help others and keep my thoughts positive. Today, I am proud to say the tenacity that got me through this challenging time has propelled my business to new levels of success.

There is no rule book for being a business owner. It takes grit, courage, perseverance, faith, and tenacity. I've realized being tenacious means never being satisfied with the status quo. In the past three years, in addition to speaking around the United States and providing one-day

Breakthrough Experiences to help business owners achieve new levels of personal and professional success, I've become an International Best-selling Author, presented to one thousand people in Las Vegas, launched a podcast called *Winning In Business*, and learned to play golf. I will continue to live outside my comfort zone with the internal agreement that my faith, family, and health come before my business.

Our society is really good at encouraging high performers to succeed, hustle, and grind for success. We are not good at teaching high achievers how to check in with themselves to see if they are living a healthy and sustainable life, or to stop and recognize the signs of oncoming burnout. Here are three critical action steps to ensure your tenacious personality is also linked to the longevity of your health and success:

1. Break through your inner chaos and gain mental and emotional clarity. Inner chaos—faulty thinking, heightened negative emotions, self-doubt—creates a lack of focus and follow-through impacting productivity, momentum, and financial success.

2. Be aware of your stress personalities. Who you are being is more important than what you are doing. Recognize what triggers your stress personalities so you can challenge the behavior and thinking of how you are acting.

3. Hire a coach. You will never be able to see your own blind spots. A coach will hold you accountable when you are not putting yourself first and encourage you to reach your goals in a healthy and sustainable way. Without a coach, chances are you will keep pushing and striving, making success more important than the self.

My tenacity to persevere has allowed me to restore my health and grow my business. It has allowed me to impact more lives across the United States, and opportunities keep presenting themselves to make a greater impact. I believe I am the success factor in my life and remain open to possibilities with outcomes that aren't always under my control. I have turned my tenacity into my testimony. I encourage you to do the same.

Kelli Risse is passionate about helping organizations, teams, and individuals break through stress, overwhelm, and old mind patterns to live more joyful and fulfilled lives. Through her speaking presentations, along with her proven coaching methods and life changing One-Day Breakthrough Experiences, she has helped thousands of people shift out of stress patterns and into better health, happiness, and financial success. Kelli's expertise is derived from being an entrepreneur in the wellness industry for more than twelve years, plus her two master coaching certifications specializing in neuroscience, mindset, communication, and behaviors. Kelli has been featured on ABC, NBC, FOX, and CBS, as well as many other online media outlets. Kelli is the CEO of Rise Up and Live Wellness, a contributing author in the Amazon International Bestseller Fearless and Fabulous, and podcast host of Winning in Business. Kelli resides in Missouri with her husband and two sons.

Kathy Lambert

Threads of Tenacity…Empowering Women to Forge New Paths

In the tapestry of our lives, it is the threads of tenacity that weave our stories together, creating a beautiful fabric of endurance, empowerment, and transformation of our souls.

– Kathy Lambert

In 1997, I read an article about Dress for Success New York. It was a non-profit organization providing suits to women transitioning from life-scarring situations including homelessness, domestic violence, incarceration, and generational poverty, empowering them to be on the same playing field as everyone else. I put the article away thinking someday it would be wonderful to do. I needed to make money. I didn't have time and didn't know anything about starting a nonprofit. God sure has a sense of humor. You see, I was searching at the time for what God wanted me to do with my life. I would wake up in the night thinking about this article. During the day, it was as if someone had their hand on my back pushing me toward giving suits to women. I finally showed the article to my husband, Brad, and without hesitation, he said, "You need to do this. You've been praying for God to show you. Here it is!" That was the beginning of Dress for Success Midwest.

Over the years, there have been many stories of women who seeded into my life and became a part of my journey. In the tapestry of my life (as I reflected in my quote, above), threads of tenacity are woven together with each strand representing women from different backgrounds, ethnicities, and cultures who taught me about resilience, determination, courage, and the willingness to keep pushing forward. Each one added a heart print on my life.

Cultivating Tenacity Through Self-Empowerment

Her name was Bridget, and she was homeless, thirty years old, and a single mom with two small children. She had a job interview and nothing to wear but a T-shirt, sweatpants, and tennis shoes. I had just picked up my first donation of suits, which were in the trunk of my car.

Bridget came from a homeless shelter and met me in the parking lot of our church. She had an interview for a receptionist position in two hours and needed something professional to wear. I opened my trunk and was so excited to find a beautiful suit in her size! We went into the church for Bridget to try on the suit. When she walked out of the restroom stall, she had the biggest smile on her face. Her shoulders were back, her head was up, and she beamed with confidence! I looked at her shoes. I thought to myself, "She can't go to the interview with a beautiful suit and tennis shoes, what can I do?" Then I blurted out, "What size shoes do you wear?" I don't know where that came from; I didn't have any shoes with me! She responded, "Size six." That was my size! I was wearing new shoes: red patent leather pumps! If you're like me, you love your shoes! This conflict went on in my head, with one side shouting "Give her your shoes!" and the other side shouting "No!" I didn't know what to do! Then the answer hit me like lightning. I took my shoes off and gave them to Bridget...And guess what? They fit!

As she looked in the mirror, tears ran down her face. I thought I offended her by giving her my shoes and told her I was sorry. As Bridget walked toward the mirror, she had her arm stretched out and said, "You didn't offend me. I have never seen myself look like this before. I have to touch the mirror to make sure it's me."

My heart was exploding. This was a Cinderella moment! Rather than a prince riding in to save her, Bridget was saving herself. She left looking and feeling different than ever before. Two hours later she landed the job!

My life trajectory changed that day. Witnessing Bridget find her strength, self-confidence, and unwavering determination to secure that job demonstrated the transformational power of empowerment for women. It was her tenacity! It not only transformed her life but also impacted her children for a brighter future. My intention was to get Dress for Success Midwest launched and have someone else take it over. However, I was immediately inspired and committed to help other women like Bridgett, believing that everyone deserves to have the life they've always dreamed of. Bridgett taught me tenacity through self-empowerment!

Nurturing Tenacity for Lasting Change

She always wore a hat and had impeccable taste, elegance, and was dressed to the nines from head to shoes! I met Clare in 2000 at an event where she was speaking about women, finance, and economic independence. I was captivated by Clare. She was an advocate for women and minorities and served at the federal and diplomatic levels of our government. She talked about what it takes for a single mom to move forward and break out of our welfare system. Everything she said resonated with me, and I knew needed to get to know her. I had learned that we can give a woman a suit. There was much more that needed to be done, however, and Clare had the answers!

I invited her to our office the next day. I shared about the work we were doing with Dress for Success and Wheels for Success (the program my husband, Brad, founded) and how we needed a holistic approach for women to break out of the cycle of poverty. She looked at me and said, "You've got it!" She shared about helping women get into nontraditional jobs with higher wages, start businesses, and gain financial independence. Clare took me under her wing and invited me to Kansas City for a fund-raising luncheon to see what could be possible. She called me often to share an idea and then would say, "Now you go do it!" She worked tire-lessly to overcome obstacles and systems that kept women down. She taught me to take a stand, not to back down, and to make a way where there was no way. She invited me to political gatherings and shared how to initiate policy changes. Before I knew it, I found myself in Washington DC attending a global women's summit—a true testament to her guidance. Whenever she had an idea or discovered an opportunity for funding for a women's initiative, she would always reach out to me.

I remember the day in 2002 when Clare met me at a women's correc-tional facility. As we were walking out, she looked at me and asked, "Why are you doing this? You should be in the corporate world." I shared that it was my passion and I had to do this. Then I looked at her and asked, "Why are you doing this? You're seventy and should be retired to Florida!" Clare looked at me with a little scowl and said, "The same reason you are." Off she went, wearing her beautiful hat, all dressed up and pulling her oxygen tank. The night before Clare passed away, she was working from her hospital bed. She never gave up. She kept advocating for women until the end.

Clare demonstrated that it took tenacity to pursue your calling. When I had to make the hard call, step out of my box, and be the voice for those who didn't have a voice, I would think of her and take action! When others said I was crazy and there was no way this could be done…I would think of Clare and do it anyway!

For more than twenty-three years I kept the vision of "Breaking the Generational Cycle of Poverty" by never giving up and by taking a stand when many said I was in a tunnel. Maybe I was, but I'm so blessed today to see the results of the work we've done. Women who began with us feeling alone, hopeless, and trapped in the system are now homeowners, business owners, authors, and speakers. Their children have graduated from high school, attended college, started businesses, have their own families, and are not repeating the same cycles as before!

It takes tenacity to fulfill a dream!

Reflections on acknowledging your tenacity within you:

1. Reflect on Your Passion: What is the thing you often think about that fuels your inner fire?

2. What are you holding back from doing because of self-doubt? How can you push through that determined to do whatever it's going to take to reach your dream?

3. Think about a time when you faced obstacles and wanted to give up but didn't. What was your "why" for moving through the challenge and coming out stronger?

My wish for all who read this is to recognize the power of tenacity in you! Always remember: "You are powerful beyond measure!" (Marianne Williamson, *A Return to Love*)

A visionary CEO and social entrepreneur, Kathy Lambert embodies the belief that every individual has the capacity to be a Change Maker. Kathy's journey, championing woman empowerment and economic mobility, began in 1997 with Dress for Success Midwest, a nonprofit that empowers women to economic independence. In 2001, she and her husband, Brad, formed Connections to Success to break the generation cycles of poverty by instilling hope, resources, and a plan.

A beacon of inspiration, Kathy turned the notion of change-making into an enduring legacy of empowerment and progress. Her contributions have garnered state and national recognition, including receiving the Volunteer Service Award from President Obama in 2014, the 2021 Legacy Alumni Award from Focus St. Louis, and the 2021 Dennis Jones Foundation Philanthropic Award.

She and Brad now inspire nonprofits to diversify their funding so they can scale their social impact through KBL Impact Partners.

Kristy Barton

Survivor

For most people, the word "tenacity" implies an empowering quality. My entire life has been filled with tenacious moments, many not by choice. Being tenacious is exhausting. On the other hand, it's the only way I know how to survive.

In the year leading up to my fiftieth birthday in 2022, I had a lot going on, personally and professionally. Like many of you, I was dealing with the aftermath of the pandemic, still feeling like a new parent (even though my son was a toddler) and wondering where and how I could manage everything. I was lost. I felt defeated. Sadly, I just felt broken.

I was going to be fifty years old…half a century. What have I done in those five decades? What have I learned? What have I held onto and, in particular, what part of my childhood have I let hold me down?

As I write my chapter, my son is four years old. My husband and I adopted him as a baby. He is living proof that miracles can happen.

Childhood shapes many people's adult lives. Some for good. Others, not so much.

Looking back on my childhood, I realize I tried to forget many things that happened to me. However, my earliest childhood memories happened when I was four—the same age as my son.

I don't believe I have ever used my childhood experiences as a crutch or as a reason to become a challenging person. It's not an excuse for making bad choices, which I have. On the contrary, I have taken what happened to me as a child and ensured that I used it to become one hell of a positive person. One who is respected. A friend. A mentor. An entrepreneur. A wife. And a mommy.

Some of the people closest to me know my childhood story. There are so many memories I have buried and try not to remember. But now that I am half a century old, I must embrace my past, share my story, and feel OK with myself. I am nowhere near perfect, but I do try my best with everything.

My dad was an abusive man to me and my sister, but even worse to my mom. I would never have said those words out loud when I was younger. For me, being a child growing up in a domestic violent household meant carrying a lot of shame. My sister, my mom, and I did nothing wrong. Yet I still felt guilty.

My parents divorced when I was in second grade. At the time, we were living in Wyoming. In the middle of the night, my mom, fearing for her life and her children's lives, packed our car, left with only a few dollars in her pocket, and drove us back to our home state of Wisconsin.

When we got back to Wisconsin, we lived with my grandma. Those are some of my best childhood memories—just me, my sister Natalie, my mom, and Grandma Taylor. Living in a small town in the '80s was ideal, except if you were a child of divorce. Not many people were divorced back then. You were an outcast. So I decided quickly to tell people my dad died instead of my parents getting divorced. It wasn't difficult. These days, divorce is more common and people often continue some form of familial relationships. Not my dad. He was out of my and Natalie's lives for nearly four years—the best four years of my childhood.

Then came the spring of my fifth grade. Suddenly, my dad wanted to not only be in my and Natalie's life but he wanted my mom back too. Looking back, I feel foolish and even more guilty, telling my mom we should give my dad a chance. Who wouldn't want to get their family back together again? If only we had known what would happen.

My parents ended up remarrying. It's now the mid-1980s, and I'm growing up and becoming a teenager. Back then, my parents' marriage felt like Jr. and Sue Ellen Ewing from the drama *Dallas*. I learned very quickly that our move back with my dad was a monumental mistake.

To this day, I do not blame my mom. She did the very best she could for me and Natalie. At the same time, our lives were in flux, and my mom got very sick. She was ill for more than a year. She went to every specialist. No one could figure out what was wrong. Ultimately, they discovered my mom had a couple of autoimmune diseases, including lupus.

My life as a teenager was complicated. It's hard enough growing into adulthood, but it's even harder when you are hiding the fact you're being abused at home. I always had a smile. Inside, I was dying. I couldn't wait to go away to college. The farther away the better. I felt guilty leaving my mom and sister alone with my father. In my mind, I did not think it was fair of me to go away, but I also knew this was my way out and I had to take it.

I left my home for college, and I never went back. When I turned thirty, my parents divorced for the second and last time. During their first divorce, I didn't understand much. I was just eight years old. Now, as an adult, sadly I know more than I should.

It took my parents ten years to finalize their divorce. Why would a divorce take so long to finalize? The answer to that question is too difficult to address. What I do know is that dealing with my parents' divorce both times left an enormous hole in my heart. All my life, I felt I was *never good enough.* Those were my dad's words. I *wasn't smart enough*—more demeaning comments. I allowed his voice into my head.

A few months before I turned fifty, I decided it was time to stop letting my past control my present and my future. I have battled depression. I have battled anxiety. I have battled loss. I am a survivor.

In the summer of 2023, my little family, mom, sister Natalie, and her husband returned to Wyoming. It was not a trip I wanted to take. I hadn't been back in nearly thirty years. Wyoming had too many bad memories. I also knew this was a journey I needed to make for myself and my family. I decided that if I went back to Wyoming, it would be to make new memories, which is exactly what happened. I found myself seeing the landscape and viewing old memories with a new perspective. The trip out west was our first long trip with our son. He loved it. When we asked him what he loved about our trip, he said he loved everything, but it was the trains that captured his interest the most. We spent day after day just watching the trains and counting the cars. The trains go nonstop in Cheyenne, so he constantly had a flow of new trains to count, and he'd tell us about all the different rail cars. Seeing Cheyenne through his eyes was so healing for me. He wants to go back very soon, and now I know in my mind, and more importantly in my heart, that I can go back as well.

On reflection, my life has clearly had its ups and downs, love and loss, and love again. Now, instead of dwelling on my bad experiences, I use them as life lessons. Each day, I take my life lessons, the bad and the good, and raise my head high. I am a wife, a mother, and an entrepreneur. I am a *survivor*! And I'm much more. I am courageous and compassionate. I learned early the meaning of being tenacious, and while it may be exhausting, it is the only way I know to live my beautiful life.

Kristy Barton was born and raised in Southern Wisconsin. In middle school, her family moved to Cheyenne, Wyoming, where she lived until she went to the University of Missouri (Mizzou), earning her bachelor's degree in Broadcast Journalism with a minor in History. After college, she freelanced until she landed her dream job in St. Louis, Missouri, to set up an in-house public relations department for a local union with a staff of one. As PR Director for eighteen years, Kristy also developed and maintained a monthly magazine, creating slogans that would be trademarked. She also helped raise substantial funds for numerous charities and organizations.

In 2015, Kristy started her own business: Sunshine Multimedia Consultants—a full-service PR/marketing firm. The first year was rough, but by year two Kristy had made a name for herself throughout the community, winning numerous awards, including the Webster Groves/Shrewsbury/ Rock Hill Area Chamber of Commerce Outstanding New Chamber Member, and back-to-back awards from *Small Business Monthly* for being one of the Top 20 Best PR Firms in St. Louis. In 2019, Kristy stepped out of her comfort zone and began gaining national clients. At the start of the pandemic in 2020, Kristy landed her first national client based out of California. By the end of 2021, Kristy was managing clients in all four time zones throughout the United States and working with Fortune 100 and 500 companies. While she may be dealing with many larger clients now, she has never stopped helping her local clients and charities back home in St. Louis.

Lynnea Brumbaugh, PhD

Is it Tenacity or Terror?

Do you remember, dear reader, the woman who did this? Who made international news in 2010 when she sent her orphan son back? Put him on a plane and sent him back to Russia?

Every one of my friends called: "I thought of you!" I could *hear* how wide and serious their eyes were on the other end of the phone. And I would howl with laughter. I felt compassion for this woman—I truly did. "Lady, look…I totally get it. We *all* fantasize about it; you just don't actually *do* it!"

I really thought this was tenacity. You do six impossible things before breakfast because you've made a promise to a child. You push through because tenacity is right and brave. Because *not*-tenacity is cowardice and wrong.

Looking back now, though, I see things differently. I see a young woman living an adrenaline-fueled life, gripped with terror that she had made an unfixable mistake. She believed she was being tenacious. And she was not entirely wrong. The whole thing did begin with tenacity, after all. Tenacity in the form of a promise: *I will not abandon you.*

It is 2002. We are standing in a Russian courtroom, tearfully telling the judge how much we want to be this boy's parents. In Russia, *Vladimir* is a grown-up name. For a child, it is sweetened to *Volodya, Vladya, Vovochka...*

Or in our son's case, *Vova.*

His back, curved from severe scoliosis, undulates when he runs. His arms are mesmerizing. No elbow joint on one arm, and this curved little wrist-like finger on the other. People might be cruel, so I have to be especially loving. I tell the judge that eight-year-old Vova will have a bedroom set that once belonged to my father's mother. My husband speaks some Russian words and then chokes up. The judge's eyes grow moist. The courtroom is charged with love, thick with the sweetness of completing an enormous good.

And then it is done, and we are in our hotel room. My husband is getting ready for a walk. It will be the first time I am alone with my new son, who thinks that I am Baba Yaga, the witch from Russian folklore who lives in a chicken-legged house.

The door clicks behind my husband. The boy *erupts*! He *screams* and pummels the bed, the floor, the walls. He hurls himself—hard!— against the thick window. I don't *think* the window will break. I'm pretty sure, in fact. But this is a disturbingly suicidal kind of action, and I don't want it to escalate.

I draw my son away from the window and toward a set of Matry-oshka nesting dolls. Palpably grateful, he immerses himself in play. The largest doll—the outer one—Vova promptly names *Papa.* The second largest is *Mama. Vova* is next. *Harper*, the baby sister waiting for him in St. Louis, is fourth. (At some point the next day, I will notice the mama Matryoshka doll missing. I will find it in the toe of Papa's shoe. *Oh, really?* I will think at my new son. *You don't want "Mama" in the family?* Hmmph. I pull myself out of my husband's shoe and place me right back in the family of nesting dolls. *Gloves on, son. I'm not going anywhere!*)

My husband returns and love-bombs his special son. We all play hide-and-seek, my son and husband adorably both in matching white undies, at my son's insistence. I draw a warm bubble bath, and Vova is a happy dolphin, splashing and laughing the song of himself. I am in love. Out of my league. An ocean beyond exhausted.

That night, we sit together, my husband and I, in a window seat that overlooks Red Square. I am suddenly struck with the enormity of what we have done, the unchangeableness of it. At this very moment, my husband turns and reveals to me a creeping disgust for the clinginess of his new son. I go numb. I would love to receive even a fraction of the affection our son lavishes on his new papa. I look at my husband slant-wise, feeling for the familiar, tender beam of love between us—and touch a buzz of electric anger instead.

"*You wanted this so much,*" he says, with a shocking bitterness. I have never heard this tone from him, and it cuts me. I am also quietly outraged. Five months ago, my husband's tear-pooled eyes had locked on mine: "*Maybe adopting this wounded child will heal my wounded soul.*" Did he forget his own words? We *both* wanted this child.

But I do not speak my outrage. I squash my sudden terror and call it tenacity, even though it was not. It was stubbornness and enabling. And it almost destroyed me.

Years after adopting our son, my husband will tell me, tears choking his voice, that he cannot believe how bad a father he turned out to be. It was not the first time he spoke such words. But it *is* the first time that my automatic *Oh, honey, that's not true* wasn't available to me. Because now I believed him. My husband had been telling me for decades who he was: a tenacious breaker of promises. And I had been tenaciously enabling him, telling him for decades, *no, no, you are a good man.*

But he was right, and I was wrong. When Vova was having his first scoliosis surgery, my husband left the hospital. As soon as we got word that our son was under anesthesia, my husband, tight-lipped, was gone. And here is the important part: I never asked why or where he went.

When Vova was a preteen, he called me at work: *"I made a face, and Dad sent me to my room. What should I do? Wait—Dad's calling me. I gotta go."* His piping voice quavers. He is terrified. And here is the important part: I did not demand to be put on the phone with my husband and tell him to stop scaring our son. I rationalized that his parenting style was just different than mine. I was wrong about that too.

Our son grew into an angry teen. My husband was in a constant rage. Walking into our house was like being deprived of oxygen. I did not admit, even to myself, why I spent an entire summer convincing my husband to move into an apartment. I did allow myself to know that I was terrified of actual physical violence in my home. My husband finally agreed to the move, and I went weak with relief. I thought, *I will not have to choose between my husband and my son.*

Only I was wrong there too. My husband soon had an affair with a friend; within a year of our divorce, they were husband and wife. It was for me a new life, too, a huge rebirthing. I cleaned up my teaching, started a business, and took care of the kids. They both grew up, went to college, became adults.

Dear reader, I know what you want now, what you expect. You want a closing paragraph that says, "After their lives imploded, and after she put herself back together again, Lynnea and her son have a healthy relationship." This is what I want too. I promise it is. But that is not quite what happened.

My son and I tried. We really did. We went on a road trip, which was sometimes good but mostly miserable. We sang a duet together in church, and he presented me with a CD of the recording, which I listened to only once. I hired a street band to celebrate his college graduation, and he believed that I had embarrassed him on purpose. Finally, I said a confronting thing, and my son promptly blocked me on all media and got a new phone number. We were officially estranged. There really are no words to say how horrible this felt. It was bad. But after a few days of panic and pain, a tenacious truth started a firefly dance in my heart. *I did not abandon him. He is an adult who made a choice. And now my mission to mother this orphan boy, my terror that I am doing it all wrong—I get to release both of these.*

And lo, a strange new island of reality emerged. Hey! My son and I both *did* get what we wanted, mostly. My son is happy. He has a home with my parents, a job, friends, and his church. And I, too, am happy. I have space and time to build out my business, energy to fuel my one wild and wonderful life, and a rich relationship with my daughter. We might have a relationship someday, my son and I. And we might not. This is a tenacious truth, but I can breathe through it, which I could not when I was caught in the grip of terror.

Dear reader, if you take one thing away from my story, let it be this: tenacity is not a gaslighting machine, so do not use it to bulldoze through your sensitive aliveness and awareness. Tenacity is the burning fuel of life and love, which holds the fabric of this gorgeous universe together. And you—your precious, tenacious self—you are a part of all that!

Lynnea Brumbaugh, PhD, a highly regarded consultant and university professor, helps leadership teams solve complex problems without emotional turbulence. The foundation of her success with clients is her remarkable life journey. Having survived three close brushes with death before age twenty-five, Lynnea treasured her tenacity as a natural gift. But then came two challenging international adoptions and a marriage that ended in betrayal and abuse. Lynnea's life became like the phoenix, and she emerged as a force of nature, driven to learn and teach effective ways of living and working with self-awareness, healthy empathy, and emotional agility. Described by CEO Erik Frank as "a star," and as a driver of "powerful ripple effects" by Metlife Sales Director Steph Dryer, Lynnea's work is particularly valuable in the post-COVID workplace, where her research-based approach equips leaders with the essential qualities needed to thrive. Her chapter in *Tenacity* is adapted from her memoir about her marriage and two international adoptions.

Rhonda Travers

Out of Balance

My world came to a spinning halt one Saturday morning in August 2020. I went to bed Friday night excited about one of my favorite activities coming up the next morning—walking three miles with friends.

When I tried to sit up after the alarm went off at seven a.m., my eyes were rolling in every direction, I was sweating, the room was spinning, and I had no balance. I have had minor dizzy spells in the past but never experienced this feeling. It was horrifying. I laid flat on my back for two hours without moving and finally agreed to let my husband pull me out of bed as I could not sit up on my own. I wanted to throw up. My head just wouldn't stop spinning. He had to walk me to the couch because I couldn't walk on my own.

I spent the next twenty-seven months experiencing brain fog, pain in the back of my head, tingling in the face, and the constant sensation of being off balance. The intensity was different each day. I was so fortunate that I was still working from home with my corporate job, as there were many days where I was too dizzy to drive. But I kept working and "powering through." I went to specialists and was given different prescriptions that made me feel worse without resolving the symptoms. I followed programs at a dizziness institute and pain management center where

I received a few different diagnoses without finding the root cause or a resolution.

Oh, and during this time I also decided to finally pull the trigger and leave my thirty-year corporate career to pursue my dream—launching my own business that aligned my passion and purpose.

Timing is everything, right? Deciding to launch my own business in the middle of a pandemic and in the middle of a health situation may seem mistimed. However, I leveraged the tenacity within me.

Tenacity helps us have courage, control, and pursuit of our passion. Early in my adulthood, I discovered my passion for coaching, training, and helping others. It all started with my enjoyment of conversations.

As a college senior completing an accounting major and studying for my CPA, I attended a networking event, had great conversations about internal audit from professionals, and was invited to an interview the next day. This changed the trajectory of my career from pursuing the popular path of public accounting to a profession that wasn't as widely known back in the 90s: internal audit and consulting.

Throughout my career, I enjoyed hiring, managing, and coaching hundreds of professionals. I was so energized when I gave a training presentation or when my employees achieved a career goal such as a promotion. I started researching training techniques and observing other trainers to learn more. I also valued my role consulting with business leaders, especially in the human resources area. I knew "someday" that was all I wanted to do—help organizations provide the tools, training, and support for their employees' success.

What is that passion that lights you up? Start by recognizing when you find yourself most energized, when it doesn't feel like work, or when you feel a genuine sense of purpose. Write that passion and feeling down and get curious about whether you are currently following that passion or also saying "someday."

We all go through tough things in life, and some are not visible on the surface to others. I have persevered over many obstacles both personally and professionally in my life because of my tenacity of inner strength and courage.

Professionally, I made a bold move after twenty years with one employer to explore other companies that offered growth and promotional opportunities within internal audit. I took control to learn a completely different industry while still following my passion to coach and develop others.

If it wasn't for the courage to make that bold change, I would not have hired a career coach to help me get started. A question that resonated with me asked what I would do if money wasn't an object. My answer was to launch my own training and consulting company. Yet my mindset was that "someday" that dream would be nice, but not now.

One of my thoughts holding me back was that I was the primary income source for our household. Given our choice of careers, my husband and I relied on my insurance plan, higher income, and other benefits of working in the corporate world. So it seemed impossible to launch my own business. However, that question and my response was stored in the back of my head.

Within two years of my new corporate role, the company was acquired and my department was dissolved. Instead of worrying, I relied on my inner strength and tenacity to keep focused on my dream. I knew if I could have the courage to make my prior change after twenty years, I could make another one. That question from my career coach still resonated with me. During my seven months searching for a similar corporate leadership role, I networked to learn how others transitioned from a corporate career to launch their own companies. I saved this knowledge for "someday."

What is a goal that seems like a dream and out of reach? Writing down your dream and what you think is holding you back starts bridging that gap. Then writing down your strengths and resources to overcome what you think is holding you back gives you control with that first step.

One quote I love from Jim Rohn is: "You're the average of the five people you spend the most time with." This is your tribe, your inner circle of influence. I am grateful for those in my life who gave me words of encouragement on the strengths they saw in me to follow my dream, even before I saw them myself. Soon in my new corporate role, instead of saying "someday," I started saying I had a five-year plan to launch my business. However, those around me often asked me: Why not now?

When there was a reorganization at the managerial level in my new company, I was part of the group who would no longer have a personnel team. Since my passion was for coaching others with their career development, I relied on my courage to make another change and answer the question from my circle of influence and turn my five-year plan into now.

Think about the people in your life you surround yourself with. Does your circle of influence include someone who will encourage you, inspire you, be a resource for you, as well as nudge you?

You may have heard the comparison of life to a roller coaster, where you need to buckle up for the ride. You can either scream out in fear the whole way through or hold up your hands and experience the thrill. After launching my business in 2021, my transition from a corporate leader to a business owner felt similar. It was unchartered territory. This impacted whether my day focused on fear or thrill.

Part of this ride included a self-development journey in 2022 by completing Neuro-Linguistic Programming (NLP) certifications. This training helped me with my biggest lesson about tenacity. What was truly holding me back wasn't the logistics of starting a business, or the pressure of being the only household income, or complexity of health insurance; it was how I trusted myself.

One key learning that resonates with me is that we all have the tools we need within us to be successful. I have spent years second-guessing myself instead of recognizing and relying on my strengths, expertise, and experience.

Another huge learning is there is only feedback in life and not failure. As a recovering perfectionist, keeping this perspective helps me view outcomes that did not meet my expectations as feedback to learn from instead of failures.

I also learned the impact of ignoring emotions and health symptoms. In the past, I "pushed through" both challenging personal situations and a high-stress, fast-paced corporate career. That morning in August 2020, I was completely out of balance. My body shut down and forced me to slow down and reflect.

When you feel out of alignment, take a moment to pause from your schedule, reflect on your dreams and passion, and acknowledge the emotions you are feeling.

My tenacity has helped me evolve to where I am today. By having the inner strength to make changes and trusting myself, I have aligned my passion and purpose. I am thrilled at how I am creating an impact today. And my equilibrium issues have been isolated in 2023! Yes, there are life challenges that create twists and turns like a rollercoaster. We can either resist and grip with fear or let go to experience the thrill.

By recognizing your passion and strengths and trusting yourself, you will have the courage to take control and turn your "someday" into today!

Rhonda Travers fulfills her passion for helping organizations provide tools, training, and support for their employees to be successful. As Founder & President of Travers Training & Consulting, Rhonda leverages her thirty years of corporate leadership and consulting experience to work with businesses and nonprofit organizations to increase engagement, retention, and productivity.

Rhonda is also committed to making a difference through positive community development. She has fulfilled multiple volunteer management and leadership roles for more than seventeen years.

In her spare time, Rhonda is a 5K addict who loves the adrenaline of crossing the finish line and power walking with friends. She also enjoys spending time at the Lake of the Ozarks with her husband, Paul.

After earning a Bachelor of Science in Accounting from Millikin University, Rhonda completed the Certified Internal Auditor (CIA), Certified Public Accountant (CPA), as well as Master Practitioner and Certified Trainer of Neuro-Linguistic Programming (NLP) certifications.

Dr. Amy Narishkin

Cultural Intelligence: A Quiet Tenacity

Cultural intelligence takes a quiet tenacity. It takes tenderness and time to talk with a person who seems different from you. When talking with someone different, a person can feel tongue-tied, awkward, and uncomfortable. That's certainly the way *I* felt when I entered the church fair event grounds on that late August day years ago. I could tell that being at an event so completely new for me was going to take some quiet tenacity.

The Word of Life Christian Church in North City St. Louis was hosting their annual church fair and school supply giveaway event. With all the hustle and bustle, I stood in the middle of the parking lot quietly wondering, "What can I, a White woman in an all-Black neighborhood, possibly have to offer at this event?" Sure, I was a member of the church, but not everybody at this event was a member or knew me. When my husband, Cyril, and I arrived, our fellow church members were in full swing setting up chairs, tables, grills, and tents. We greeted and hugged everyone. Then Cyril got right to work helping with setup. He's more extroverted than I am; I'm more reserved and thoughtful.

In that quiet moment, it occurred to me that whatever I did, it would be good to sit down and not stand over people. I said to myself, "OK, then where?" That's when I saw my buddy Jonathan at the entrance acting as a one-man welcoming committee. He was standing by a card table with two chairs provided for visitors to sit down and complete a short questionnaire. That's where I could sit! I sat down and watched how Jonathan so easily engaged with folks, clapping shoulders and shaking hands. He knew the language of the community and shared most of the people's skin color. Since Jonathan and I often spar and chat it up, it felt natural to help him with greeting. So I stayed there, seated at the table. It wasn't long before I noticed fellow moms, who had come for the school supplies, joining me at the table to complete the questionnaire.

As moms were bent over the table completing their questionnaires, I was at kid eye level because I was sitting down. I got to talk with their children, ask their names, and tell them mine. I learned what they thought of school; the little ones tended to enjoy school, while the teens seemed to be either proud of their efforts or frustrated with the system. As a mom and a teacher, I could relate. I shared stories about my own kids' struggles with school and tips for understanding how the system works and how to navigate it. But first I was doing some deep listening, giving them eye contact, and affirming their experience. From little ones, I'd get a hug, or sometimes we just held hands and giggled. The teens would chat me up and laugh about their experiences.

Leaving assumptions at the gate

As an educator, I'd heard that kids in the city don't always start school the first day of classes, but I didn't know why. That didn't seem right; it made me sad to think some kids would have to start the school year already behind. But that day at the card table, I left my assumptions at the gate and actively listened. Since the first day of school had been three days earlier, I asked one little girl how her first days went. She said she hadn't started school yet. The mom, who was sitting with me at the table, looked up from her questionnaire and told me she'd lost her job as a nursing assistant, so she didn't have the money for her daughter's school uniform.

I said, "I get it. I'd want my child looking prepared for school." She visibly relaxed. Jonathan overheard the conversation and offered to connect her with a friend who is a nurse to see if she could help the mom find a job. She thanked him. I told her that if she still wanted to get that uniform, the folks at church could help. Jonathan pointed to the door across the street where she could go to talk to someone who could help with the uniform.

At first my sitting there at the table seemed insignificant, but I began to see the value of it. Just sitting there communicated several things, from simply, "I'm listening up—not down—to you," to letting everybody know we were in no rush and that they mattered. I could see the impact of waiting and allowing people to reveal themselves and their needs in their time. This is how I discovered this real need for time, tenderness, and tenacity.

Another mom came in through the gate with her three teenage children, a son and two daughters. Her daughters launched into telling me all about school. As we chatted, their brother was quiet, rather stoic. I asked him how school was going. He looked down and quietly shook his head. His mom said, "He hasn't started yet. He has developmental delays. I'm worried he'll be bullied. I haven't been able to get off work to meet with the teachers."

I said, "I understand; we need our kids safe. I've got children with learning disabilities. I like to meet with the teachers too. Do you mind if I ask you a question?" She said it was OK. "Does your son have an Individualized Education Plan or IEP?" She nodded. I said, "With an IEP, you can ask to meet with his team of teachers before the school year starts. In fact, you can meet with them monthly until you're sure he's safe."

She said, "I didn't know. I appreciate that."

I said to her son, "That's got to be tough when you don't know what kids are up to." He nodded. "You can ask your teachers for help. Most teachers really want to help." He smiled.

Steps for connection

Hearing people's stories was all together heart-wrenching and heartwarming. Active listening can make tenderness bubble up, prompt us to take our time, and grow our intention to see what emerges from each conversation.

It's also a bit unnerving not knowing how or where a conversation is going. To connect with someone who we perceive to be different takes intention and a determination to see the other's dignity. This is particularly true when one person, like me, is from an historically more powerful cultural group attempting to connect with a person from an historically marginalized group. This is the case for a White person talking with a Black person, a man talking with a woman, or an adult talking with a child.

A culturally intelligent person, who finds themselves in a situation where their color, background, or other factor(s) put them in a position where they're more powerful, must double their efforts to prove they are worthy of trust. They know that it's not just them, the individual, talking; rather it's them plus all those cultural factors and history that are talking.

If I'd come in hot with my assumptions, biases, and opinions—or even talking *at* someone because I'm just curious and not thinking about the impact of my open curiosity—*that* posture would have shut people down. When you take the time to connect with a quiet tenacity, recognizing people are tender beings, people are much more likely to open up and genuinely share.

With cultural intelligence, there are seven steps I've learned to use to connect with just about anyone who has a different background or perspective:

1. Slow down, take a breath, and withhold assumptions.
2. Check my intention: is this person an object of curiosity or am I interested in a genuine human connection?
3. Be willing to let the conversation go.
4. Share something about yourself to show your vulnerability.
5. Ask them about their experience.
6. Listen deeply.
7. Affirm their experience and feelings, even if it's different from your own.

When we pursue a genuine human connection, we discover we and the other person both have something to learn. If we're willing to deeply listen, we're both changed and benefited. This posture of willingness to learn is more productive than assuming we know the problem and the solution. It brings about clarity as well as buy-in and mutual commitment toward bringing about the solution.

Organizational leaders, too, can allow the true needs of current and potential clients to come to the surface using these seven steps. For their employees, they can model and encourage collaborative leadership skills by stepping back, being present through deep listening, and letting others describe how and what is needed in the existing situation. It's with this quiet tenacity that we create safe companies and communities where everyone feels like they belong.

Retention and engagement are at an all-time low; leaders must create a culture of safety and belonging. With a PhD in Adult Education and thirty years' experience, Dr. Amy Narishkin is a consultant, strategist, and executive coach helping organizations across multiple industries, including financial, healthcare, construction, and manufacturing, make the shift to Cultural Intelligence. Dr. Amy is the CEO of Empowering Partners, LLC. She has worked domestically and internationally with more than four hundred leaders—CEOs, Executive Directors, and management teams—to effectively increase their ability to lead, retain, and engage people who have different perspectives and backgrounds. Dr. Amy leverages a globally recognized tool for measuring ability to navigate cross-cultural conversations, the Intercultural Development Inventory® (IDI®), for which she is certified to administrator. She regularly receives over 90 percent "exceeds expectations" from the programs she conducts. As a cross-cultural thought leader and successful entrepreneur, she empowers leaders to create an environment where everyone feels valued, heard, seen, and engaged.

Heather Budwell

Dig Deep

All I could hear was the pounding of my heart like a bass drum in my head as the second hand ticked closer to two p.m. I rubbed my tiny, sweaty hands on my corduroy overalls and tried to breathe deep. I prayed she wouldn't call my name today, but like most days, she said, "Heather, would you take paragraph two, please?" Heat rose up my neck to my ears as the words swirled on the page like a bowl of alphabet soup. I tried my best to decipher the chaos out loud, but it always ended in a tongue-twisted mess with my classmates giggling at me behind their papers. It wasn't until I was nine years old that I was officially diagnosed with dyslexia. Even at that young age, I knew I needed to dig deep and pull out a powerful energy and drive to keep up with my peers academically. In my child's mind, I birthed a new friend who would always be with me. She would cheer me on during those challenging moments and give me the unwavering resolve to face and overcome the adversity and obstacles that would try to tear me down throughout my life. I named her Tenacity.

In college I pursued a degree in interior design, as I do have a natural eye and love to create beautiful things and spaces. My senior year I attended a study abroad program at the American College in London, England. Thanks to my very loving and generous parents, I was able to study architectural preservation in London and surrounding countries. We visited

Switzerland on a field trip, and I clearly remember cautiously climbing out to an overlook point and soaking in the vast, breathtaking views of the Swiss Alps. It was at that moment that I had a profound experience, and I heard my lifelong friend, Tenacity, challenge me: "This is it," she said. "Your life is before you now. Who do you want to be? What kind of life do you want to live? It may be hard, but you can do this! Don't let anyone or anything stop you from creating the most adventurous life imaginable." I took a deep breath of the pure mountain-crisp air and chose a life of fortitude and resolve. Tenacity has always been there to gently push to take the next step or to accept the next challenge. She has relentlessly fought to instill in me the confidence to do hard things. She has taught me to dig deep. In that moment I believed I could do anything I set my mind to and that I could do it well.

Difficulties, changing circumstances, setbacks, and obstacles have not been a stranger to me in life. After graduating college, I chose a career as a corporate interior designer in the office furniture dealership world. Space planning corporate floorplans and designing furniture layouts became my specialty. Eventually I met my husband, and we had three children. After the birth of my firstborn we decided it would be best for me to stay home to help raise our family. After the children were all in school, I started my own interior design business. I helped remodel kitchens, bathrooms, and basements. Business boomed and I was thriving until the day the rug got pulled so hard out from under my feet it almost broke my back. I discovered my husband was having an affair, and when confronted, he chose to leave our family and pursue a new life with another woman.

My world was absolutely shattered. I was so devastated I did not have the physical or emotional compacity to continue serving my clients, let alone take care of my own children, who desperately needed me. I was riddled with fear, imagining how my world would change, and the uncertainty of raising three children on my own. How could I be tossed aside like a piece of trash after sixteen years of marriage and three beautiful children? The rejection, abandonment, disrespect, and dishonesty I endured was horrific and traumatic. I was so wrecked that my mother-in-law had to take my kids back-to-school shopping because I could barely function. I was paralyzed in crippling pain, and it was time to dig deep once again so I called upon my lifelong companion, Tenacity. She challenged me to draw on that inner strength and determination I breathed in on that Swiss mountaintop. I was determined to rise above my circumstances and create a new life for myself and my children. I had to change my mindset from that of a victim to that of a champion!

I had been out of the corporate world for eleven years while I raised my kids and ran my business. After my divorce was finalized, I needed health insurance and to find a new home for my family. The devastating loss of my business in the divorce meant that path was no longer an option. I had poured myself into building my company and had developed strong relationships with contractors and clients. Walking away from it felt like I was losing a piece of my heart again. I had no option but to return to the workplace.

I was unable to reenter as an interior designer. The computer programs and design software the industry now used was foreign to me. I was a quick and eager learner, but no one wanted to hire someone who needed training. I had to pivot and create a new approach to be attractive to an employer. I implored my guide, Tenacity, to aid me once again in taking a self-analysis of the talents and skills I had developed as a business owner, and to see how I could market myself to reenter the workplace. I realized I am very well suited to be a business development manager. I have an authentic desire to develop and grow relationships, and I am also a natural connector of people. Eventually, I was offered an opportunity to join an office furniture dealership as a workplace consultant/business developer. I started to develop and grow a network of women who support and help each other in business. We share business leads and offer encouragement to one another. They are, to this day, my ride or die tribe, my CREW.

Now, I have been focusing on business development for almost eight years, and most recently I had the opportunity to work in that role for an incredible architecture firm in downtown Saint Louis, Missouri. This role feels like I am coming full circle to my original love of architecture (without all the math)! I am very blessed to be able to say I love what I do for a living. I believe I am making an impact and difference in the lives of those I touch throughout my day.

My children are thriving and making their way into the world. I am happy to say they have each incorporated Tenacity into their lives, and I have seen them dig deep to accomplish big things. My oldest son is a junior at West Point Military Academy in New York, my daughter is a freshman in college seeking a degree in business and entrepreneurship, and my youngest son is a senior in high school, who was recently accepted to Missouri State University for a degree in theater education. It has not been an easy road for the four of us, but we have endured and overcome so much together and have had a lot of fun and laughs along the way.

Living as a professional adult with a learning disability has had its challenges, but being able to lean on my old friend, Tenacity, has served me well over the years. Together we have embraced challenges and adversity as opportunities for growth and refinement, while maintaining a strong sense of purpose and drive. Tenacity has given me the strength and determination to cultivate resilience and perseverance when rugs get pulled from under my feet. Tenacity has empowered me to dig deep and believe that I can and will live the most amazingly adventurous life possible.

So, to offer you a step-by-step approach to adopting Tenacity into your life so that you can live a life of resilience and success, I challenge you to do the following:

1. Embrace Life's Challenges and Adversity as Opportunities for Growth and Rediscovery of your Dreams. An unwanted moment for recalibration. This is your True North moment.

2. Own a Willingness to Embrace Obstacles and Hardships as stepping stones toward creating an adventurous life, no matter how painful the process may be. Allow yourself to dream big on how your life can look and go after it!

3. Adopt a Growth Mindset. Understand that achieving success often requires sustained effort even when facing setbacks. This is where you need to dig deep to find that drive and motivation to get back up and keep pressing forward. Your effort here is a path to mastery.

4. Maintain a Strong Sense of Purpose and Motivation. Develop a clear vision of what you want to achieve and how you want to design your life. Be passionate about your goals and do not let anything distract you from achieving that vision of a new reality.

5. Cultivate of Life of Perseverance and Resilience. Resilience allows you to bounce back from setbacks, adapt to changing circumstances, and maintain a positive mindset. Perseverance, on the other hand, is the commitment to staying on the course and not giving up in the face of obstacles or failures.

Being the connector that I am, I am happy to have introduced you to my lifelong friend, Tenacity. I know once you get acquainted you will reap the benefits of a life full of resilience, passion, and drive, and indeed live the most adventurous life imaginable! Go crush it, friend! You got this!

Heather Budwell is the Business Development Manager at FGM Architects in Saint Louis, Missouri. With more than twenty-seven years of experience in the architecture and design industry, including owning her own interior design and home staging business, she has a passion for connecting people and ideas through creative and collaborative solutions. Heather is involved in several industry-related networking organizations, of which she serves on leadership levels including CREW-St. Louis, SMPS, SLC3, and SICHE.

Heather has a passion for helping others and fighting for the voiceless. She is the founder of The SOLD Project-St. Louis, a local nonprofit organization that raises education and awareness for domestic minor sex trafficking. Heather is a thriving single mother of three amazing young adults. She enjoys traveling, kayaking, hiking, listening to live music, and attending festivals. She especially loves to smile and laugh with family and friends.

Alison Engelhardt

Both

Have you ever had seemingly impossible days, weeks, months, even years? When getting out of bed was anguish? And yet you pushed through. Or perhaps reading this book is your first step in that effort. Conquering struggle is not step one on the path to achieve tenacity. How you persevere amidst struggle *is* your tenacity. Give it time, keep your tenacious eyes open, and read on for some examples of how the counterintuitive "both" have found their way into my reality.

"Dad! Someone is trying to break in!"

"Honey, it's an earthquake—go back to bed."

"Dad! This is no time for jokes!!"

"No, honey, really—it's an earthquake. You can go back to bed. Love you!"

"What?! Weird. Thanks, Dad. Love you too!"

April 18, 2008, 4:37 a.m. Not the place or time to expect an earthquake in St. Louis, and certainly not how I expect to kick off my Friday. Following the earthquake, I embark on an otherwise normal workday at my entry-level commercial real estate job. That is until I return to the apartment, ready for the weekend.

The front door cracked open, quietly creaking in the wind. I walk in and find a cord graveyard scattered across the main floor of the townhouse. The new flat-screen television is missing.

Again, following my twenty-three-year-old logic, there's only one person who can help this make sense:

"Dad, did you borrow my TV?!"

"Huh?"

"I just got home from work, and the door was open. The TV was gone. Did you borrow it?"

"Ali, get out of there and call the police! We're on our way."

The early-morning earthquake conversation with Dad was highly improbable foreshadowing: my door had been crowbarred open; someone broke in. According to the police, my roommate and I (along with several neighbors) had been watched and were now the victims of theft.

I temporarily relocated to my parents' house and eventually returned to my apartment and its unbreakable lease. I spent several months swimming in the void left by my previous faith in humanity. Gradually, a hesitant but self-curious smirk found its way across my face: Why did I *know* someone was breaking in that morning? Later that same day, why did I *not know* someone *actually* broke in?

Eventually, I was able to see it: I effortlessly made deductions based on what I knew. I *knew* my second-floor bedroom shook when someone used the front door. I *knew* coming home to an open front door was highly unusual. I *knew* I just dropped my savings into a fancy flatscreen TV. I *knew* my dad could be a jokester. I then took my rock-solid knowledge and effortlessly constructed convicted, confident, undisputable, *blatantly wrong* facts that shaped my decision to walk through the front door. That decision could have led to a more dangerous outcome, but thankfully it left me only with contemplation.

I did not initially leave space for other possibilities beyond my "facts." I did not question my response in either situation. Granted, an earth-quake or burglary aren't ideal times to pause and pontificate about the profound depths of "why," but the experience left me with a challenge. What happens when I pause and intentionally make space to consider: *What if things aren't what they seem? What if I'm wrong? What happens when I intentionally strive to extrapolate facts from assumptions?*

Q: Why did I call Dad, anyway? Both times. Why Dad? Dad certainly didn't expect an early-morning Midwestern earthquake! And let's be honest, the break-in was probably *more* of a surprise to Dad than me (Dad didn't need to see the open door and technology-vacant apartment to inform his response, not to mention he probably— unlike me—would have noticed the splintered doorframe).

A: I called Dad because I knew Dad would help.

Q: What did I expect Dad to do? He couldn't erase the earthquake from history. He couldn't prevent the break-in or become a save-my-girl's-stuff vigilante.

A: He didn't have to fix the situation to help me.

Q: So, how could Dad help?

A: Resolving and fixing are not synonymous. Dad was a quiet master of unassuming resolution.

Dad was not blinded by the glamor or expectations of perpetual growth mindsets and constant need to carpe diem. Instead, Dad quietly permitted, validated the moments between. In this situation, these were the moments between the break-in and when I was ready to take my next step. While Dad was larger-than-life, fun, and jovial, he very much normalized space for the unfun, uncomfortable feelings. He made both spaces, and everything in between, perfect in their own rights.

In the days and weeks following the burglary, I was not OK. Dad did not rush me past the pain. He buckled in for the long but real journey of finding solid ground. He never told me how to heal; he was just there, reinforcing that—whatever I chose for my next step—I could do it. I was not broken, just hurt. And I, with time, would find a way to heal forward. Until then, though, it was OK—in fact, it was its own perfect—to spend time with my fear, uncertainty, and insecurity. The honesty and validation of that human experience didn't return my stolen things, but it helped me find peace. Finding peace was step one to finding resolution. What's more, I received a very unlikely gift: a chance to struggle and find new confidence and power throughout and on the other side.

Since that time, I've grown to embrace the blessings in my life differently—my family, friends, faith, career—with more gratitude. Amidst the joy and gratitude, though, the pain and consequence of April 18th have found me on many different dates and in many different shapes. The lessons of April 18th, though, have rooted me in the space for both joy and pain.

Later in my twenties, I survived an assault that left me with a severe head injury. After regaining my mental capacity, I spent time recollecting the days following the theft—the now-familiar hopelessness and the long journey to feeling OK again, and the far-sweeping dread that came over me—and knew the journey to healing would be harder this time. I then remembered I didn't need to be perfectly healed to find joy. Thank God the assault did not take my life or physical ability, so I committed—in that moment of realization—to the journey. I gave myself permission for both: bad and good days. Pain and joy. Weakness and strength. Vulnerability and power.

After my body healed and I spent quality time seeking emotional help (folks—please get therapy if you think you might need it!), I eventually found the counterbalance to the bad, pain, weakness, vulnerability. I found my Both. The assault was not my choice. The injury was not my choice. But I no longer felt like a victim; I was a warrior. I was not—and never will be—the same person I was before the assault. But I found my good, my joy, my strength, my power. Relentless perseverance is often the product of challenges and struggle, fighting through struggles and intentionally reflecting, self-challenging along the way. Struggle is not the opposite of tenacious resiliency; it is tenacity's necessary but repulsive fertilizer.

I also moved on to find my husband and start our family. The biggest joys in my life.

June 2016: I sat at home eating a delivered pizza with my husband while I finished several quarter-end reports for work. Our four-month-old son had just fallen asleep. The phone rang: Dad fell at work, and an ambulance was bringing him to the hospital. I met Mom and my sister at the hospital, where we learned Dad didn't fall. He passed.

I paced the halls of the hospital sobbing, mentally pleading to wake up from this cruelest nightmare, grasping this new reality: life as I knew it was over. I *knew* I would never find joy again. My closest friend, biggest fan, and strongest pillar was gone. A big part of me was forever gone too. How could go I on?

Dad's wake brought a seemingly infinite line of people impacted by Dad. Then his funeral. I didn't sleep or eat for days. I lost my ability to connect to anyone—including myself. The grief suffocated my waking and dreaming moments. My soul ached.

Five days after losing Dad was the longest time I had ever gone without talking to him. I struggled knowing day six and day seven would soon follow. Day six did, in fact, come. As did day seven. And year six. And year seven.

And time continues to pass. And grief remains. A part of me died with Dad that night, but what I *knew* that night in the hospital hasn't held true. I have found joy again.

Dad survives in me. Amidst the grief, I find gratitude for the love. I am beyond blessed to have a dad whose life I see in every moment. Every immature joke…every Christmas tree…every time I look beneath the surface…every struggle that begs my company…every time I survive.

Since that time, I've found new blessings: My second child, morning visits with Mom, new friendships, and an altered gratitude for the life around me. Pain and struggle happen, but they gift us the building blocks to tenacious perseverance; they provide a battlefield to exercise growth, gratitude, intentionality, and resilience.

Sure, I've seen pain. So have you. I have also seen joy. So have you. The pain does not preclude tenacity; both pain and tenacity often converge on the same battlefield. I challenge you to find and permit your own tenacity—not outside of your struggles, but within them. Take root in your Both.

Alison Engelhardt is a *Women We Admire*'s Top 50 Women Leaders in Finance and a *St. Louis Business Journal* 30 under 30. Her career takes root in relationship management, economic development, and tax credit equity. Alison helmed six successful New Markets Tax Credits applications, resulting in $270MM tax credit authority to benefit low-income communities throughout the country. She served eight years at U.S. Bank, most recently as Vice President for their Environmental Finance group, where she managed a team overseeing $3B dedicated to renewable energy assets. Alison now serves on Steadfast City Economic & Community Partners' leadership team, working closely with professionals from diverse skill sets who share the singular goal of developing better.

Although Alison takes pride in her career, no accomplishment overshadows her greatest joy: space and time with family and friends. Alison most enjoys playing games and creating LEGO worlds with her two young sons.

Kelly Quinn

Nanny Nanny Nou Nou

When you think about iconic nannies, women and characters like Mary Poppins and Maria from *The Sound of Music* come to mind. They epitomized everything that children need: curiosity, grace, gentleness, love, adventure, relentlessness, and tenacity. These two wondrous caregivers were often at odds with the children's parents over their style of caregiving, and with the children themselves. It wouldn't have been surprising if either quit before the job was done, yet neither ever surrendered the white flag. They remained committed, compassionate, and confident in their craft.

When I accepted the glorious opportunity to serve as a nanny in 2004, these two characters were ever present in my mind. I longed to be playful and adventurous while also being firm with boundaries and expectations. As a young woman in her twenties, the real nannying experience was far from how I envisioned it from the movies, yet the journey proved to be significantly influential in shaping me into the woman I am today.

I had recently graduated from college and was eager to pursue a serious career in hospitality; you know, because I majored in it and knew everything already…The opportunity to serve as a nanny was unexpected and honestly was not my first choice—by a long shot. What I did recognize was the opportunity to earn money and have free time during the school day to continue my search for the "perfect job."

After the first few weeks, my job search efforts dwindled. Taking care of three school-aged kids took a lot of effort and time management. I became awestruck as to how parents got their kids from activity to activity and made sure there was food to eat, clean clothes to wear, cozy beds to sleep in, and everything else that seemed to magically appear in my current life up to that point.

Caring for three kids was really hard and kind of terrifying. I often thought about how I had no real qualifications to be a nanny. I hadn't gone to "nanny school," yet all of the sudden I was responsible for other people's kids, and not like a babysitter kind of responsibility, but seriously responsible for their lives.

I wondered to myself, "Who thought this was a good idea? Who believed I was qualified for this? How did this happen?"

Answer: "I'm an impostor and haven't been found out yet."

I reflected on my newly minted "nanny" impostor role and hyped myself up by saying this in my mind: "I'm in this now, and I am not a quitter. Procrastinator, yes. Quitter, no. Honor the commitment and do your best; stay tenacious in your efforts. They are counting on you."

Fast-forward through the first year, and I realized that I was not an impostor after all. I actually knew what I was doing and had all of the qualifications.

My teenage jobs as a lifeguard taught me how to be prepared and how to calmly respond in an emergency situation. I used this skill in the first month when the oldest child was in a serious car accident that resulted in a few broken bones and several months of physical therapy. Majoring in Hotel and Restaurant Management gave me the knowledge to prepare nutritious, budget-friendly meals, and to value the importance of keeping a tidy and clean house while remaining kind and courteous.

Most significant on the list of qualifications was being raised by a remarkable mom who made it all seem like everything in our lives magically happened, and who passed that finesse on to my sisters and me. Believe me, for those of you who have been blessed to have Nancy in your lives, you understand. She has a radiance that shines on everyone with a fierceness that lets you know she is the boss.

So how does the story end? It hasn't.

Nearly twenty years later, the family I nannied for and I have celebrated life together, and some momentous occasions. Like the time we moved to Luxembourg for four years, and I became affectionately known as the "Nou Nou" (pronounced "new new"), French for "nanny." We've celebrated graduations and witnessed a soldier head off to war and return home. We've danced the night away at weddings, shared awe at the birth of our own children, and through it all we remain close and forever connected. We remain family.

It's humbling to reflect on how it started and how it's going. There were countless moments when I felt defeated, conflicted, uncertain, lonely, desperate, and frustrated along the journey. It was at those crossroads when I had to choose to face the moment and either wave the white flag or keep on pushing through the hard stuff. I had to dig deep and persevere with grit and tenacity so the good stuff could be revealed.

As you read my story, I challenge you to reflect back on a moment that you felt marred and deflated, when you were at a crossroads in life and you chose to keep going. You chose to trudge tenaciously through the quicksand because you knew that, on the other side, the purpose of the journey would be revealed joyfully.

Choose the hard stuff. Choose to refuse defeat. Choose to show your tenacity, and you, too, will look back twenty years or more from now with a full heart and joyfully exclaim, "Nanny. Nanny. Nou Nou."

Kelly Quinn is a tenacious community connector who strives to influence transformational change that betters lives.

Currently Kelly serves in a development role with the Alzheimer's Association where she pursues partnerships to elevate awareness and education of dementia through the wide range of services offered via the Association.

Previously, Kelly discovered her superpowers at TinySuperheroes (TSH) as the Director of Programs. She tenaciously applied her passion to help people discover a sense of purpose and belonging.

Kelly's Superpowers are Patience, Positivity, and Perseverance.

Her Kryptonite: Onions and mean people.

Kelly garners nearly two decades of nonprofit leadership, development, and management experience. Highlights include serving people with intellectual and developmental disabilities through Best Buddies International and the Pujols Family Foundation.

When she's not tenaciously pursuing transformational change in the community, she is with her family. She married her soulmate, Ryan. They have two curious and adventurous sons, Harry and Eddie. She enjoys being walked by their goldendoodle, Jerry. The Quinns love their family tradition—Friday Pizza & Movie Night!

Katie McGovern

Authentically Tenacious

Tenacity.

According to Merriam Webster Dictionary, to be tenacious is to be "persistent in maintaining, adhering to, or seeking something valued or desired." Synonyms for tenacious include strong, sturdy, and tough, "showing power to resist or to endure."

When I think of tenacious people, many come to mind. Single parents who do it all. People living with chronic or fatal disease. Minority business professionals. People who walk unabashedly in their faith. True to the definition, these people show determination in their quest for balance, for normalcy, for equality. They are strong, sturdy, and tough.

But am I tenacious? I had to dig deep for this one. I wanted to find some defining characteristics that represented me.

As I reflected more on the meaning of tenacity, another aspect of the definition became clear. Tenacity may come naturally for some, but it's also nurtured. Tenacious people don't always have it easy. Tenacious people work hard, knowing how to channel hardships into resiliency, and then to use that resiliency to drive them.

This thought pattern was starting to resonate.

My husband and I welcomed our first child, Megan, in November of 2010. Megan was a healthy baby, and we spent the first eight months of her life figuring out how to be new parents. We balanced successful careers with playdates, walks around parks, and the occasional babysitter to remind us of earlier years.

In July of 2011, I had finished a long work week and was eagerly waiting for my husband to return from a work trip so our family could regroup and relax for the upcoming weekend. Late that afternoon, I got a call from our day care provider saying that Megan was vomiting profusely and was more lethargic than any sick child she had seen. Panicky, I rushed home and called the doctor, who said we should continue to watch it as it could be a normal stomach virus.

Over the next two days, things didn't improve, and we went to the emergency room not once but twice. The first time was to replenish Megan's fluids. The second time was about twelve hours later, and she was noticeably agitated. Something wasn't right. Back in the ER, we were expediated to the attending doctor who scooped Megan up and, with a team, completed x-rays, blood draws, MRIs, and finally a spinal tap that confirmed the unthinkable: bacterial meningitis.

Bacterial meningitis. What? Why? How? These were some of the questions we asked during our stay at St. Louis Children's Hospital. There was no clear explanation. In rare occasions, the pneumococcal germ can bypass the ears, nose, or throat, where it usually causes illness, and make its way to the brain and spinal fluid. We didn't know at that moment, but we were facing a life-or-death situation.

Throughout the next month, Megan had extended fevers, seizures, and strokes. We were routinely consulted by internal medicine, infectious disease, neurology, neurosurgery, and audiology. The nursing staff was incredible, giving us information and space when we needed it.

Megan slowly began to heal, and with the support of our pediatrician, we were able to leave the hospital. We were advised that there would likely be long-term implications of the disease and time would tell. Immediately, though, we faced a new set of challenges, such as helping Megan regain strength to eat, sit, and crawl. A shunt was placed in her brain to help drain fluid. Hearing loss was monitored while she regained strength.

At ten months of age, Megan had an auditory brainstem response (*ABR*) *test,* which is the most conclusive way to confirm hearing loss. My husband and I believed that she had at least some natural hearing. She turned when we walked into a room and seemed responsive to oral stimuli.

The test came back conclusive—profound hearing loss. She couldn't hear anything. You could put a jet engine to her head, and she would only feel vibrations. *Your daughter is deaf,* they told us.

Our family was stunned. We didn't know anything about deafness or hearing loss. I laid in bed for a week and cried, mourning a future I had once envisioned and trying to prepare for a different version.

Megan is now twelve years old. She attended the Moog Center for Deaf Education through kindergarten and then joined a mainstream classroom with support from Special School District. She wears bilateral cochlear implants and is fluent in American Sign Language, which she uses daily to navigate the world. She loves dog walking and participates in diving, soccer, and her middle school softball team.

As a family, we participate in hearing and d/Deaf communities, which allows Megan access to all, and gives our family opportunities to learn and understand. This has been instrumental in my own growth and confidence, helping me embrace myself unapologetically while becoming a fierce advocate for others who don't always fit in.

Megan's illness is a decade behind us, but the journey continues daily, and I am profoundly shaped by it. The experience helped me understand the fragility of life. I had to accept that things don't always go as planned.

And I learned the importance of being vulnerable and meeting yourself, and others, where you are.

For me, tenacity has come by channeling these lessons and using them to help navigate everyday situations. I approach my personal and work life through the following lenses:

People come first. No matter the circumstances, we are imperfect humans, and we need each other. We had incredible support when Megan was sick, and we still do now. When we experience life's rawest moments together, amazing things happen—communities rally, friendships rekindle, and passions are reborn.

Recognizing the human connection has greatly enhanced my leadership. By accepting that emotion is part of our work, employees can come to the office with personal ups and downs, strengths and weaknesses. When you allow for open dialogue and support of those things, you can build trusting, confident relationships and teams. And in turn, those team members care deeply about their role in the organization and do great things. I am relentless in building teams who share these values.

Be Bold. Boldness is a kickstand to tenacity, and being bold takes courage. In *Daring Greatly* (2015) Brene Brown says, *"Courage starts with showing up and letting ourselves be seen."* It took some time for me to get comfortable with this concept, and to stop worrying about what other people think of me and my family's needs. A breakthrough was when Megan began to participate in organized activities. To this day, I routinely work with businesses to provide interpreters, advocate for that service, and educate coaches and friends on how to work with people who are deaf. Those who are deaf are truly the experts on this front; however, I can attest that it can be hard, tiresome, unaccepting, and frustrating work. It's important, though, because while it helps our family, it also paves the way for the next person. Advocacy has allowed me to stand up tall with a strong voice, become a strong negotiator and progressive decision-maker, and an overall more confident business leader.

If you want to experiment with tenacity, try stepping out of your comfort zone. Speak up in that meeting. Throw your name in the hat for PTO president. Tell someone you care about them. Maybe it works out, maybe it doesn't. In the end you tried it, and without doubt, you have gained something from the experience.

Find the Solution. Marie Forleo says, "Everything is figure-out-able." I am a firm believer in this concept and that every problem has a solution. It might mean a twist on a desired or planned outcome, or a completely new direction, but if you work for it, there is an answer.

Embracing this mindset has been the biggest game changer for me when it comes to managing challenges personally and professionally. When something heavy hits, I sit in the emotion for bit, while recognizing that this is a moment in time and answers are imminent. This can be so tough—messing up a project, getting a call from a principal about your kid, losing someone you love. It might not feel like it, but all these situations have a next step. Some are immediate, some may be longer term, but with the help of good decision-making, all lead back to the path of stability.

I reflect often about our family's journey and how it felt like things would never be normal. But then I look at the now—a new normal—where I have a great career, am continuously learning American Sign Language, enjoy a full community of peers, colleagues, and d/Deaf friends, and so much more. It's not what I expected, and there are still bumps in the road, but it's truly a blessed and amazing life.

This chapter on tenacity wouldn't be complete without crediting the queen of tenaciousness, my mother. If you need a nonrefundable airline ticket refunded, a plumber at your door in an hour, or scones (well, that credit goes to my father) on your doorstep, you know who to call. My tenacious mindset was shaped early on by my mother's get-it-done attitude, coupled with deep care for people, something shared deeply by my father. Mom and Dad, this chapter is dedicated to you.

Note: d/Deaf is a term that describes two communities: "deaf" or "d" refers to people who are deaf audiologically and are comfortable participating in the hearing world through lip reading, speaking, and hearing devices. People who identify as "Deaf", with a "D," see themselves culturally as part of the Deaf community. In Deaf communities, deafness is seen as an innate part of self. Typically, members will not wear hearing devices and American Sign Language is used as the primary language.

Katie McGovern is a twenty-plus-year veteran of the St. Louis nonprofit community, working in the areas of fund development and executive leadership. She has spent the last decade serving the mission of The ALS Association, where throughout her tenure she has increased revenue 110 percent in the St. Louis market. Katie is often recognized for her business acumen combined with a personal, authentic approach, helping build strong, productive relationships and teams. She has been honored with several Innovation Awards and the Mentor of the Year Award through The Young Nonprofit Professional Network (YNPN). Katie has held positions on local and national committees with the ALS Association, and within the community. She is passionate about women's leadership and has served on the Girls in the Know board of directors, while routinely supporting activities and programs for the deaf and the Deaf communities. Katie lives in St. Louis, loves the outdoors, and enjoys spending time with her husband and three kids, Megan, Matthew, and Molly.

Rhoda Banks

I Grew Up in the Ghetto. So What?!

Growing up in the inner city of downtown St. Louis, under the authority of a single parent and as the oldest of four girls, is not for the faint of heart. My life's journey, like others, came with its fair share of challenges. I've come to believe that hard knocks, trying scenarios, unfair treatment, and being overlooked in the workplace and often unseen will breed and activate tenacity—if one does not faint.

As an only child until the age of five, I was the center of attention for the adults who resided in our concrete-based floor and lead-paint-peeling apartment. I had no idea we were poor. I learned during my freshman year of high school that not only were we poor but that I lived in the ghetto.

This lesson came after becoming friends with a girl at my high school. I invited her to spend the night at my house after I had spent the night at hers. We had so much fun making homemade donuts using canned biscuits. We roamed the neighborhood, and I introduced her to my friends.

On Monday, I returned to school to discover that I was the butt end of my classmates' jokes. They blurted, "Rhoda lives in the ghetto!" and the class roared with laughter at my expense. The young lady who I thought was a friend was not, and she had told anyone who would listen all about where we lived, nicknaming it the "ghetto." They knew all about our concrete floors, the lead-based paint peeling off the walls, and the not-so-pleasant ambiance of the place I called home. I felt betrayed and hurt, but I knew I had to endure the ridicule if I wanted to remain in that school and secure a quality education.

My mom, although challenged mentally, emotionally, and financially, sacrificed to send my little sisters and me to a private grade school. From that experience, I wanted to go to the private high school where all my grade school friends were going. My high school experience showed me how mentally and emotionally strong I was, even as a younger person. After witnessing murders, watching my stepfather beat my mom, waking up to a knife held to my throat by my mentally unstable mother, and being told on multiple occasions that I was ugly, I tenaciously held my own and focused on my goals for a better life.

Who am I?

I am a woman who has leveraged adversity as fuel and motivation to propel me forward. I walk and live in a state of great determination. I have committed my life to helping others do the same. I am determined to leave a legacy of helping others win. I have been through rough times, many of which affected my confidence and how I viewed myself, but all have contributed to the woman I am today.

I am the offspring of a mother who never experienced a healthy version of parental love, and therefore did not know how to display healthy parental love to her four daughters. I do not recall my mother ever uttering the words "I love you." She never knew her father, and her mother was an alcoholic for the early years of her life. I am the child of an assassin. My father was a member of a popular gang in the 60s and early 70s. I am also an individual who was determined to prove wrong that old saying, "the apple doesn't fall far from the tree."

I have been working since the age of fourteen. My very first job was with the St. Louis Agency on Training & Education (SLATE). They provided eight-week summer jobs for underprivileged youth who lived in the inner city of St. Louis. I worked every summer until I aged out of the program, and I used the money to buy school clothes for myself and my three younger sisters. My high school counselor told me that, according to my test results, I would struggle in college. According to her, my trajectory included being a social worker. I thought to myself as a senior in high school, "What's a social worker?"

The morning of my sixteenth birthday, my mother woke me up before she left for work and sternly told me that if I did not have a job by the end of the day I could no longer live there. I got dressed and walked the entire downtown area applying for jobs all day. My final stop was Burger King. I completed the application, and the manager looked it over and said, "You're hired. Come in tomorrow for orientation." I was ecstatic! I worked at Burger King for four years, all through high school, and purchased my very first car during that time.

After a short time in college, I thought I had really moved up in life when I got a job at a large hospital system as a cashier in the parking garage, and later transferred to patient transport as a telephone operator. I was married by this time with my firstborn son, and we could barely eat we were so poor. I later transferred to the billing office at the hospital as a customer service representative. My coworkers bullied me because my manager praised my high performance. Their taunting and nasty remarks made me cry. One day, a manager took me to her office and said, "Rhoda, these girls are jealous of you. Dry your eyes and recognize that you have the ability to make a lot of money one day." I have never forgotten her words.

While working in another part of the same healthcare system, my leader said to me, "Rhoda, you have so much potential. I see you as an executive one day. Have you ever thought about going back to school to get your degree?"

I had not thought about college after dropping out, getting married, and raising my firstborn son. Her question inspired me to enroll, but I couldn't afford the books for my first class. So I paused my efforts to return to school. Later, that same leader followed up with me and asked if I had enrolled in college yet. I said I would have to wait because I did not have the money for books. She paid for them on my behalf.

My first class was Communications, and I got a C even though I'd earned a higher grade. I challenged the teacher about my grade, and he explained that only a certain number of students would get an A, a certain number a B, and the remaining students would get a C. No matter how hard I worked, he saw me as a C student. His limited vision of my academic abilities only inspired me to earn all A's going forward. I did! I graduated cum laude with a bachelor's in business, and later earned two master's degrees with honors.

My tenacity helped me make it out of the ghetto and excel in life. I was determined to do this not only for myself but so that I could one day help others. I want those who had a similar path in life to know that they, too, can defy the odds and achieve the highest level of success they desire.

In my life's journey, I have learned that the only person who can stand in my way is me. I have crossed paths with people who cared enough about me to speak words of encouragement and affirmation to me. I eventually believed them, and they followed up those words with action.

What does it take to win?

To win, it takes pure ability, which everyone has, and it takes uncompromising determination. In addition to these very foundational winning ingredients, it often takes one person caring enough about another person to help those individuals recognize their unique gifts and talents, hone them, lean into their natural abilities, and create opportunities for them to excel.

The level of trauma I have experienced contributes to the deep care and concern I have for others. Yes, I grew up in the ghetto. So what?! Where I started is not where I will end. Where I lived as a child does not define me, but it shaped my perspectives and my persistence. Tenacity fueled me to build a better life for myself and to help others to do the same.

I encourage and challenge all mankind to go after greatness, not just for self-gratification but to positively influence others and be a role model. We all can demonstrate that no matter what life throws at you, no matter how bad the hand you were dealt, you can go as far as your faith, tenacity, and passion will take you. To those people who have had a hard past and who may be living in a hard present, know this: when you put your mind to something, it will happen. Hard work, tenacity, and integrity are my priority values. But the highest value I hold is to serve others. I have realized my purpose, and that realization requires me to strive for greatness. One cannot be a blessing to others if they themselves are not blessed.

Rhoda Banks grew up in the inner city of downtown St. Louis and currently serves as the Executive Head of Culture & Inclusion for American AgCredit. She has a reputation for being a high energy, enthusiastic, and strategic developer of others, and for converting "no-win" situations into "win-win" success stories.

Rhoda is active in the community, serving as a board member for St. Louis Community College Foundations, a mentor for the St. Louis Organizational Development Network, and an adjunct instructor for Webster University. She is a sought-after speaker and published author of an inspirational devotional journal: *Moments Stories and Words to Inspire, Confront, and Conquer Everyday Life Situations*. Rhoda is also a proud alumnus of the *That's What She Said* St. Louis cast.

Rhoda holds a bachelor's degree in Business Administration (cum laude) from Lindenwood University, a master's degree in Human Resource Training and Development, and a second master's degree in Healthcare Administration, both from Webster University.

Erika Z. Schenk

Triumph Through Tenacity

"She's quite tenacious, isn't she?" I overheard these words spoken by the head of school to my junior high counselor, Mrs. R, as I left her office. I had no idea what the word meant, and, perhaps due to the general insecurity I felt in those awkward adolescent years, assumed it wasn't a compliment. This wasn't the last time I would hear someone use the word "tenacious" to describe me. I'm guessing it also wasn't the first, but it is the first I recall.

In the weeks before, I ran for Student Council Vice President at my school in Indonesia, where we had lived for many years. My friends tried to talk me out of running because as a seventh grader running against a popular eighth grader, the odds were not with me. But I wouldn't be dissuaded. I poured all my energy into campaigning, making posters, canvasing the student body at lunch, and setting up ad hoc "town halls" in the locker huts around campus. I had stickers and buttons that said "Erika for VP," which I would press into the hands of anyone who would listen—or in some cases unsuspecting passersby. By the end of the second week, my campaign was gaining momentum. It would all lead up to the student council speech and debate assembly where all the candidates would stand and deliver their campaign speeches and respond to questions. The weekend before the assembly, I made my family listen to my speech at least two dozen times to make sure it was perfect.

Sunday night, I finally took a break. A friend asked me to go roller skating. Of course! (It was the 80s after all.) Maybe it was lack of sleep from working on and worrying about my speech all weekend, or maybe a little hubris about my chances of success the next day, but clearly I felt a little more daring than usual because rather than sticking to our usual, safe, and mostly flat path, my friend Sasha and I attempted a skate up and down a (too steep and not really meant for roller skating) incline. I don't know exactly how it started, but soon I was tumbling and ultimately landed with my right leg not where it should be. An ambulance, X-rays, and ultimately a cast. It was broken. My mom said I couldn't go to school the next day as the cast was temporary (it was made with bandages soaked in plaster) and we needed to fly to Singapore urgently to see an orthopedist to have it set properly. I refused to miss the speeches and begged my mom to delay our flight until later in the day so I could deliver my speech. Monday morning, I hobbled onto the stage (on crutches) and delivered my (slightly revised) election speech at the student body assembly, boldly proclaiming, "As you can see, I need your support." The crowd erupted. In the days after, I became a minor celebrity among the junior high.

The day of the election came, and votes were tallied. I lost. By four votes. Losing by such a small margin was hard to accept. I insisted Mrs. R recount the votes—which she did—only to confirm the count. I remember coming home with kerosene emotions in search of a match to find release. My mom would not indulge me. She told me, "Erika, you didn't gain the title of Vice President, but you didn't lose anything." She turned the narrative away from the loss of an election to my hard work, perseverance, and determination. She told me I didn't need to hold the title of Student Council Vice President to make an impact.

That night I found myself energized and more determined than ever. With that fire lit, I went to work. My parents connected me with a local distributor that would donate bags of Famous Amos cookies. I petitioned the administration to allow me to sell the items on school property, even though I was not part of any official student-body organization. It took a few tries, including convincing Mrs. R to be my faculty sponsor and convincing the head of school that I would be accountable for all inventory and proceeds. To this day, I'm not sure if I convinced her or just exhausted her. But in the end, she approved my fundraiser, and we raised around $2,500 USD for Ethiopian relief.

Fast-forwarding many years into my law career, I found myself working at a large law firm, enduring the grind that comes with being a "big law" associate. I approached my work life just as I had my school life. Work hard. Learn the material. Do the assignment. Get a good grade. Advance to the next thing. The formula worked in school, and, seemingly, it was working in the real world too. I was taking on increasingly complex assignments, being entrusted to handle matters on my own, and exceeding the billable hour expectations that came with the job. My annual reviews were all positive. So when I walked into the last review I would have prior to being put "up" for partner, I was not prepared to hear I would be passed over.

Much of the meeting is a blur, as is often the case when you are taken off guard with unwelcome news. My file was "missing" specific credit allocation for incoming work that would support my candidacy. My contributions were largely unknown and unnoticed. I spent years working hard on projects and achieving results but never asked for credit or promoted my achievements, so others were able to take credit for them. Later I would learn that my lack of self-advocacy allowed a different narrative to be told—one that downplayed my contributions and allowed others to remain in the spotlight.

I walked out of the meeting angry, and in an instant I was transformed into that awkward seventh grader trying to find my way out of defeat. My friends took me to lunch and gave me the space to be angry and hurt, but also reminded me of what I had to offer. I left the office early that day, and my mom was once again there to set me back on track. She reminded me of all the effort I had put into helping the firm and its clients. I needed to decide what I wanted for my future, and if that was to stay with the firm and make partner, I had to learn the rules of the game I was playing. I felt some of my mentors had failed me by not counseling me on the need to show specific kinds of credit "on paper," but, in all fairness, I never asked. I assumed the "good student" approach (head down, do good work, get good results) was enough. It wasn't. I failed to advocate for myself and take ownership of my career. I had placed it in other people's hands and assumed that if I took care of the work and achieved results, they would reward me for it. They didn't. I could assign blame and never move forward, or take ownership of my role.

By the next day, I had made up my mind. I wanted to make partner. To do that, I needed a clear understanding of the criteria against which I would be measured, which I requested of management. Nothing could be left to chance. Over the next year, I met with dozens of partners around the firm, outlining my objective and asking them, when the time came, to advocate for my work and accomplishments and to support my promotion. It wasn't easy. It was a hard-fought battle requiring direct and uncomfortable conversations with some who were not interested in sharing the spotlight, even where deserved. I needed to demonstrate the support of clients and ensure that the credit systems at the firm reflected my contribution. This was a campaign—one I was determined not to lose.

The day the firm announced my partnership was one of the highlights of my professional career, but not for the reasons I might have thought before the journey began. It wasn't about the title or prestige. This was my accomplishment. A validation of my tenacity, drive, and determination to define my career. A proclamation to the world that I could and would fight for myself, and win.

I'm not sure if calling seventh-grade me "tenacious" was meant as a warning or compliment. I want to think it was the latter. Either way, I have embraced tenacity as a guiding principle that propels me forward. I encourage you to do the same. Tenacity acts as a force multiplier, fueling your confidence and inspiring others to join you along the way. When faced with a setback, personal or professional, take the moment you need to acknowledge the disappointment. Feel the hurt. Cry if you need to. But don't indulge it too long. Remember the importance of self-advocacy; humility does not require invisibility. Focus on where you want to go, summon your tenacious spirit, and enjoy the journey.

Erika Z. Schenk serves as General Counsel & EVP of Compliance at World Wide Technology. In this role, she leads global legal and compliance, as well as government affairs, environmental, health & safety, and Environmental, Social & Governance strategy and reporting. Erika is a "third-culture kid," having spent most of her formative years in Indonesia where she attended the Jakarta International School. Her mother immigrated to the United States from Hungary, and the combination of her European heritage and her time in Asia fueled her passion for travel and learning about other cultures. Erika graduated first in her class at St. Louis University School of Law. Prior to law school, Erika earned her degree in broadcast journalism at the University of Missouri–Columbia. During college, she worked part time at the local NBC affiliate as both a reporter and producer. Erika and her husband live in Labadie, Missouri, with their two teenage boys. They have two dogs and keep bees and a few dozen cattle.

Sarah LeMoyne-Davidson

Failing Forward

Young Sarah

Sarah LeMoyne was the ideal firstborn child. She was heavily involved in sports and activities throughout high school and college, had a solid group of friends, and, for the most part, excelled at anything she put her mind to. She was also fairly naïve and sheltered, thought she knew best like most young adults, and wore a pair of rose-colored glasses. She was the first person in her immediate family to go to college and was accepted into every college she applied to. She didn't stretch herself, and really saw nothing not go her way. By the end of college, she had a solid boyfriend, a fantastic internship, a full-time job opportunity, a blooming career awaiting her, and big aspirations. She "had it all" while continuing to do everything she was "supposed" to do—go to college, get a good job, find a man, get married. Sarah always worked hard and hustled for as long as she could remember. As a child, she sold lemonade and handmade bracelets; as a teen, she sold homework; she worked multiple jobs and was determined as hell. But she didn't really know what for.

Eight years later, she was not the individual you would have expected. Instead, you would have found Sarah Davidson on the floor in an oversized suburban home, inconsolable, with her post-partum depression through the roof and her marriage over. All this, while still trying to maintain her full-time career, be present to her two daughters who were under the age of three, and keep her struggles a secret. She did not tell a soul; no one in her immediate circle had failed at a marriage, nor had their life crumbling around them, and she didn't want to be the first. She couldn't fail; she hadn't worked this hard for all to explode around her. But it did.

That was me.

In hindsight, I fought ridiculously hard to hold onto a marriage on the premise of "what should be." It took me years to realize that I had lost myself. The bright-eyed, driven, fun-loving Sarah LeMoyne was gone. I'll never forget my best friend pulling me aside and saying, "Where in the hell did Sarah LeMoyne go? She wouldn't respond like this; she wouldn't allow this. You need to find her."

Over the next few years, I rode the wildest rollercoaster of my life and learned so many incredible lessons.

Finding Tenacity

When I lost myself and became a shell of a human, the internal strength I possessed, the passion I had for life, and the image of incessantly attempting perfection disappeared. My body resembled an ailing and decrepit woman, and I was fueled solely by my daughters, Skinny Pop, and Coca-Cola, and a need to relentlessly seek answers to questions no one really could answer. In these moments, I had to do things I had never done before, and I was so uncomfortable and embarrassed.

I was shaking as I called my boss from my car in my therapist's parking lot and told her about my situation. She met me with more grace and understanding than I could have ever imagined; she provided me with resources, an open ear and heart, and the flexibility I needed at that point in my life. Over time, my boss became my friend and a sponsor for me in my company.

When I told my team of two, I wrote an email to let them know what was really going on, hit send, and literally ran out the door. I refused to even look at my emails that evening. When I arrived the next morning, I received beautiful notes from both of my team members, and they shared their own personal experiences that I was unaware of. I was always so focused on work that I neglected one of the most important parts of being a good leader: really knowing my people. I have never forgotten that day and how they made me feel, and I am forever indebted to them.

I selectively told others, and although not everyone had the same response, I quickly learned who my true friends were. From there, I spent countless hours in therapy, trying to find myself and be a better human, mom, coworker, and friend. I also sought counsel from anyone I found to be trustworthy, and relentlessly shared in the hopes of finding the perfect answers, the golden key to all my problems. I exhausted everyone around me, including me. What I learned, though, is I had people in my life who never gave up on me: dear friends who let me stay in their spare bedroom and kept me occupied whenever my girls were with their father; and my parents, who let my girls and I move back in when I had spent nearly one year putting offers in on houses to no avail until I found one. I had friends who would show up on my doorstep with food, and no matter how draining I was, they loved and supported me unconditionally.

Post-divorce and acclimation, I came out stronger and better than ever, much like the infamous phoenix reference in the book *Night of a Thousand Thoughts*: "On your way to greatness, you will fall, but like a phoenix rising from the ashes, you too shall rise again." I was tenacious and did just that.

As I grew stronger physically, mentally, and emotionally, I knew that everything that had happened was a gift, and I was ready to accept it.

Through determination and strength, I began to do all the things I wanted to do:

- I continued therapy to focus on being the best mom, friend, and coworker I could be and went through my company's executive leadership development program, which was therapeutic in a different way This program will forever hold a special place in my heart because of the deep self-assessment, reflection, and growth it gave me.

- I took amazing trips around the world, went to music festivals and danced with a free heart, erased the boundaries I had unnecessarily put up, and created new boundaries to protect myself, while exploring the world with a new viewpoint.

- I began to look more closely and intently at all the things I wanted to do that would fill my cup, support my sweet little family, and help me continue to grow personally and professionally.

I was continuing to reach new peaks, and I was so proud of how far I had come. My girls were doing well, I was very happy with my career and company, and then the world shut down when the pandemic hit. Like many human resource professionals, our day-to-day worlds, as we knew them, were flipped upside down. In addition to our daily responsibilities, we now also had to manage the impacts of the pandemic. Like many women, we were now homeschooling our children. In typical fashion, I buckled down and did it, though sometimes it was a minute at a time. However, in my traditional spirit, that wasn't enough—I had always wanted to go back and finish my MBA that I had started many years ago. With no social time and limited distractions, I applied and was accepted at Saint Louis University.

Two and a half short years later, I graduated with an even greater perspective on life and a 4.0 GPA. I did it. Two months later, I was promoted and received the coveted invitation to partner at the very company that supported me personally and professionally through the worst of times and the best of times.

Lessons from My Story

I believe sharing our authentic and honest stories is one of the most powerful ways for others to learn. At this stage of my life, my advice to you is:

- Prioritize your mental health and yourself.

- Write down your aspirations and goals and take time to create your plan to make them happen; the onus is on you. Remember, they won't always happen immediately; take them one day at a time, one month at a time, one season at a time, and only look back to see how far you have come.

- Identify sponsors at your company and in your community who will support and champion you, who will uphold you when you are not in the room and provide you honest feedback in the spirit of supporting your growth, development, and success.

- Find and cherish your people and nurture those relationships. You will need them, and they will need you. In addition, there is no shame in being candid or your authentic self when you are with them—it will be respected and appreciated. If you can't be, then you need to find new people.

- It's OK to change and evolve. Young Sarah worked hard to ensure she never failed, but she had no idea that you could, in fact, fail forward and be so much better for it.

Sarah LeMoyne-Davidson, PHR, SHRM-CP is Vice President of Human Resources at Roeslein & Associates, an international engineering, manufacturing, and construction firm. When Sarah joined in 2013, they had two hundred employees; today, they have grown to twelve entities, 1,200+ employees, and have no plans to slow down. Based on her contributions at Roeslein, Sarah won the 2020 Human Resources Award from the *St. Louis Business Journal.*

Prior to Roeslein, Sarah served in HR and safety leadership positions with manufacturing, logistics, and environmental companies throughout the Midwest. She holds her PHR, SHRM-CP, California micro-credential with SHRM, a BS in Management with an emphasis in Human Resources, and an MBA from Saint Louis University.

In addition to her professional achievements, Sarah has a passion for connecting with people and empowering them to accomplish their goals, giving back to the community, and, most importantly, being a mom to her two daughters, Hannah and Charlotte.

Samantha Menezes

Dark Eyeshadow

Life is a series of chapters. Some chapters are quiet, and their pages turn quickly; a few are happy and joyful memories. Then there is the one chapter that makes you stop and think and pivot. For me this series of events is that life turn.

It was a regular workday, but my eye was not seeming quite right. I assumed it was a bad contact lens, so I switched lenses and waited a day. My eyesight did not improve, so I called my regular eye doctor who sent me to a specialist. I walked into the clinic in my red printed skirt, cream blouse, and brown jacket complete with brown boots, dressed for work. In my car was my laptop bag and lunch. Why lunch, you might ask? I planned to see the doctor and then go to work.

The doctor walked in and took about two minutes to look at my eye. He went back out and returned with a grim expression. "Is it bad?" I asked. He said yes and referred me to a retina surgeon, saying I needed to get there right away. "Do I have time to go home?" I asked, and he said, "No," there was no time to be wasted. Being the independent person I am, I decided to drive there with dilated eyes. About one mile away, I turned back and asked the receptionist to call me a taxi. Thirty minutes later I was at the retina surgeon with my husband. I still had my laptop

223

and lunch with me. It seems like something I wanted to hold on to and get back to my normal day.

The diagnosis: a detached retina. There were a couple of surgical options available. I chose the option that would require a second surgery as we were flying out to Hawaii the next week for a family vacation. This surgery would heal the eye, but I needed another surgery to remove the piece they put in to heal the eye. I would not be able to see clearly with that eye during the vacation. We made it work with several fancy sunglasses and a lot of holding hands.

When situations like this happen, we google our symptoms. I did too. A lot of people have detached retinas, but they are older than me. I would be fine, I thought. I was determined that this would be a tiny blip in my life. I only had to hang on until the next surgery and life would be back to normal. A few months later, all went well with the planned surgery. A few more weeks and I would be back to normal. The end was in sight, or so I thought. Little did I know this was the beginning of one of the toughest life lessons I would learn. I would have to rely on my tenacious self to pull me through.

A day later my retina detached again. We drove to the emergency room in the dead of night. They confirmed a detachment and asked me to come back in the morning to meet with the surgeon. At our morning meeting, the surgeon said emergency surgery was necessary. I waited another five hours for him to be available, and I was back again in the operating theatre. I was back to square one with the first of two surgeries, again. A few months later, I was back for the planned surgery. My sight could not be restored completely, but they had done what they could. As I recovered, I had to sleep upright in a recliner for days. Although at the time I did not understand, please know that God had a plan.

Then another twist: all these surgeries caused a cataract. So, to the cataract surgeon we go to schedule a cataract surgery, followed by a couple of laser surgeries. Picking a cataract plan for surgery is complicated. It only sounds easy.

All these months, I had to stay home for a week after each surgery. I had restrictions on carrying anything heavy and working out. While I continued to work, I still wondered if I would ever be normal again. Seven surgeries later, I still didn't know if I would drive again or be able to walk on a trail alone. I must admit, I lost courage and determination for a while. Giving up would have been easy.

But then something clicked, and I was determined not to give up. I saw the support of my village and how everyone rallied around me. I could overcome this and get back to work, learn to walk alone, and drive without complete vision and perception. Most importantly, I learned that it was time to drop friends who were not really my friends. You don't need to call your friends for help. They help when help is needed. I remember each one who went out of their way to help me. Life is short, and it is important to speak your mind.

I still wake up in the morning and remember that I cannot see well. In the end, tenacity kicks in to help us move on and thrive with our life changes. It is easy to tell someone who is suffering to be tenacious, that you need to set your mind to it. It will not make you happy automatically. If you want to recover from a traumatic episode, you can do it. People will say mean things and you must ignore those. The eye is a tiny part of our body but oh so complicated. Do not underestimate its intricateness. Also, the eye surgeons are crazy good.

It is important to have a few circles of friends to lean on. Each circle has a different theme and friends with different skills. Each set of friends has a different learning, and it is important to learn from them. They enhance your determination and can help you grow in each area of your life.

Sometime the people who you say a casual "hello" to will be the ones who step up to help without being asked. I recall each and every person who helped me each step of the way. If someone is driving slower than you think they should, that's OK; maybe they cannot see well (at least that's what I choose to think). Life is short, and it is important to speak your mind. I am grateful for my family and friends who held my hand during this time, and I am also thankful for the ones who I could not lean on so I can move forward without them.

What I lost on this journey was being able to see clearly with both eyes. I lost a few people who I thought were my friends. What I gained was lifelong friends, and I became more determined than I have ever had to be, more aggressive; and look at my goals for the next twenty years. I'm not ready to share those just yet. That will be another chapter in another book.

Finally, why is this chapter entitled "Dark eye Shadow"? As you have read in the above paragraphs, I had several eye surgeries. One of the after-effects is that my eyelids are not aligned, and while this condition could be fixed with plastic surgery, I chose not to have another one. I had had enough. When I wear dark eye shadow, I see this condition more clearly. It is a reminder of the months of surgeries and recoveries. It reminds me to be determined, overcome setbacks, and move on.

Be your tenacious self and own your story.

Born and educated in Mumbai, India, Samantha Menezes came to the United States with a job in IT consulting. She is a member of Women in Technology and has led the Women Employee Resource Group and the Diversity Group during the course of her career. She recently changed careers from consulting to working in healthcare technology at the Cigna Group.

Samantha sits on the executive nonprofit board for Rung for Women and is active in social justice causes at her church. She is passionate about mentoring professionals who are starting their careers. Samantha loves to travel and has run several half-marathons. She lives in St. Louis with her husband, and their two grown sons are in college.

Leenna Choudharry

Tenacity Takes Her Beyond Expectations

When I was invited to write this chapter, I googled the word "tenacity" to get the exact definition: "tenacity means mental or moral strength to resist opposition, danger, or hardship."

Welcome to my world. Although I may appear vastly different from you, dear reader, in race, gender, profession and education, what unites us is the fact that, ultimately, we all face the same issues in this mortal world. We all inhabit a world that is full of expectations and is results-driven, where all of us are racing to achieve our goals while running away from our fears.

Growing up in India, I was surrounded by family, friends, and social circles. With multigenerational families in Indian culture, the norm is always about setting an expectation of accepted behavior. These norms for each member of the family are based on hierarchy, then using role models from society and family members, parents are grooming the next generation to fill in those roles when the time comes. I was groomed as well from childhood, but deep down I was always seeking the truth of who I am and the purpose of my life. I wondered, "Am I what people around me tell me I am, or am I destined for living a life of dignity and peace, capable of something totally different in life?" Luckily for me, my dad never said what was right and wrong, but he always encouraged me to seek the truth on my own, to learn new things, read, and meet people.

Carrying the burden of being a perfect child for my family, living the perfect Indian American life, marriage and motherhood life moved fast for me. Through these roles, I often wondered who I was and where I was heading. The complexity of each life phase and my decisions in those moments were always made based on what people would think of me and the expected standards of behavior. I excelled in those roles, always for the world, but my inner struggle to seek the real purpose and freedom did not pause. I made innumerable sacrifices for my career, health, and happiness in order to fit into those roles for others.

On airplanes we're instructed: "In case of turbulence, secure your air mask first before helping others." If I was in a situation to choose between mine and my loved ones' safety, I would put their mask on first, not mine, because of the ways I was raised. But there comes a time when you realize the truth that to be of help to others you must be alive and capable yourself. Finally, a time came in my life where I had to secure my mask first before helping others. With that decision, my true tenacity journey began.

The first time I migrated to the USA, I was not given a choice to make my decision but simply had to follow and dutifully adapt to my life here. However, this time around I had to make that decision knowing well that I would lose what I had built here and not have the option to go back to where I came from. I had to thrive and survive here in America with what I had. In those moments of decision-making, I had to believe in who I am and not worry about money or what people would think of me.

A few strategies that worked for me during those months of decision-making included choosing to keep an arm's length distance with the people, friends, and family who did not support me so that I stayed focused and did not doubt what I was doing. When you are fighting a war with limited resources, and the opponent has an army, you must be strategic about the use of your resources.

Being an accountant by education and a businesswoman doing this balancing act of managing with limited resources, I called on my inner strength and intuition to be my guides to success. I leaned on friends and mentors who had been through those situations and asked for their advice.

When I finally broke the glass ceiling, it was a new beginning, and not just for me. I also broke a lot of cultural barriers, and I set a new norm for other Asian American women, helping them to know there is no shame in doing what I did, and that it is an acceptable way of life. Going forward, I had to decide my priorities and focus on securing myself in every way. Then the pandemic hit.

As an Asian American minority woman rediscovering business needs during the pandemic, and realigning my life goals with my career goals, a lot of resources and support were needed to pull me through. Growing the business with the goal of gaining new clients was a challenge for me since I am not a pushy salesman. Growing up in a culture where you are always expected to give rather than ask for what you need, it was difficult to go out into the business world and ask for clients to choose my company over other competitors, or to ask for better pay when I applied for jobs.

Speaking to my mentor, I realized that people saw value in me being direct and sincere; it meant I did not have to follow what everyone did with cold calling and messaging random people on social media platforms. I started to lean more on my strengths of being direct and straightforward, and success followed in every venture I took.

Being a minority woman in the business world where no one knows you and not having a proven track record to lean on, I became active in several business networks locally and nationally. In the past few years, I have gradually grown the business beyond just the local St. Louis region to national and global connections, which was possible due to the support of friends, mentors, fellow business owners, and amazing business networks.

Finally, I am on the right track both professionally and in my personal goals. Sometimes you must lose it all to gain what is truthfully yours. You must take that chance on yourself, and miracles do happen. Help comes to you from all directions that did not exist earlier. You must keep reminding yourself tomorrow is going to be better than today.

I am energized each morning for the day ahead. I make a task list only for that day, and at the end of the day see what I've accomplished. I am free, finally, to own up to my good and bad decisions. For women, we put too much burden on ourselves, not realizing that most of these expectations are wants and not needs imposed upon us by society. Often through turmoil, we move away from faith, but for me staying connected with my roots and culture, and accepting other faiths and norms, have strengthened my resolve in humanity and kindness toward others. Taking care of mental and physical wellbeing should always be a priority for us all, for women especially, so never ignore your health. My yoga teacher told me that the priority order of life should always be: health, wealth, and relationships.

Leaving precious parts of my life behind twice, and innumerable sacrifices along the way, this time I am focusing my energy and aim to have balance in my personal and professional life with love, dignity, and peace. I would say the "grass is greener on the other side" once you have discovered your tenacity and GRIT to break those barriers. Success follows in all walks of life—just be ready to embrace it and smile on the new journey ahead. Namaste.

I invite readers to connect with me, learn about my journey, and get inspired to live your life to the fullest both personally and professionally.

Leenna Choudharry is an entrepreneur, author, and speaker. She is living life to the fullest, embracing Asian American life and leading the path to success for other women to follow. Leenna is an entrepreneur engaged in managing an IT consulting company, Placement Expert USA, as well as an academic coaching business.

Her entrepreneurial career began in 2012 when she founded American College Gurus to provide personalized learning programs for students in the greater St. Louis region. Her reputation and strong work ethic led to exponential business growth across multiple endeavors. Leenna also speaks about faith and women empowerment in the business world, and she volunteers across several organizations in the St. Louis region.

Trisha Gordon

Accept the CHA-LLE-NGE: BE Tenacious

"Our steps are established by the Lord" (Psalms 37:23)

"I can do all things through Christ who strengthens me."
(Philippians 4:13)

On March 17, 1976, St. Patrick's Day, around 7:40 p.m., I was born prematurely at five and half months with an underdeveloped brain, heart, and set of lungs. I was not expected to live and was left in the hospital. A nurse named me *Trisha* in recognition of St. Patrick, which means noble and loyal. I did, however, live past the age of one, three, and five years. After a decade of adversity, I was placed in foster care. From the time I was born, I have faced challenges resulting in inevitable change. But tenacity was also given life.

I believe that every instance of change starts with a cha-LLE-nge. If we learn to tenaciously embrace challenges with a positive and growth mindset, we can get to the heart of any challenge: Live For, Let In, Excuse Yourself. This challenge will show you how to deploy these strategies and focus on opportunities that strengthen you, teach you something new, empower you to do more in life, and restore or release what is needed to move forward in life. Build energy through tenacity.

Accept the Challenge: Tenaciously Live Purposely

It was the winter of February 1987, and despite being bundled up like a mummy, it was hard to fall asleep because, without electricity, the house was cold and dark. I kept thinking about my mother. My then-sixty-year-old father had beaten my twenty-nine-year-old mother so badly she left home fearing for her life. I had not seen either one of my parents in days. I was used to my mother leaving, but she always returned. As I lay there shivering from the cold with an empty belly, I found warmth and comfort in my thoughts of her and her voice. I eventually drifted off to sleep.

Later that night, I was awakened by desperate voices shouting my name. "Trisha! Trisha!" To my dismay, it was not my mother's voice. As I struggled to get up, a cloud of smoke hit me in the face. My eyes started burning, and my eyes filled with tears. I gasped for air and suddenly realized the house was on fire.

Instantly, I remembered a teacher or firefighter chanting, "Stop, drop, and roll." Despite my heart racing with fear, I dropped to the wet, damp, cold floor, with no regard for the roaches and mice that were typically there. I could vividly hear my mother saying, "Girl, get your butt up off that nasty floor." I crawled toward the desperate cries that were my North Star to escape the burning house. I eventually reached the hand of a tenacious firefighter, who picked me up and said, "I got you." At eleven years old, navigating through a burning house fire was the biggest challenge I had faced, but I survived.

Accept the Challenge: Tenaciously Let In What You Need

For everything, there is a season and a time for every matter under heaven. (Ecclesiastes 3:1)

After the house fire, I was placed in foster care. This experience would bring one of my biggest life challenges to date. On December 24, 1987,

Christmas Eve, the house was lit up with decorations, including a bright-green Christmas tree. It was the first time in my life I'd ever decorated a Christmas tree. The aroma of the food was wonderful! There was laughter throughout the house as family members danced to the sounds of Otis Redding's "Merry Christmas Baby" and the classic sounds of Sam Cooke's "Twisting the Night Away" and Marvin Gaye's "Let's Get It On." A massive wave of nostalgia came over me: my mother listened to these same songs to numb her pain. My eyes filled with tears.

I sat alone in my room, rocking back and forth on the bed, consumed with homesickness. Like the house fire I had survived ten months prior, my mental health was on fire. Being tenacious at eleven years old was tough, and I struggled to get a handle on my feelings. I could not extinguish my mental health fire, nor did I know how to ask for help. Unlike my mother, I could not numb the pain. Later that night, I attempted to take my own life. I spent the next thirty days in a teen psychiatric ward. But help was on the way.

Accept the Challenge: Tenaciously Excuse Yourself and Manage Your Time

My mental health scare and attempt to take my life resulted from a combination of being abruptly placed in foster care, being disconnected from my parents, my feelings of abandonment, and being isolated. In the hospital, I felt even worse, and more isolated. I had been taken from my parents, and now I had been taken from the foster home. During my stay in the hospital, however, I got the help I needed. I was assigned an individual therapist and participated in group therapy sessions. I met young people whose situations were far worse than mine. These young people were unhappy with life and their hospital stay, needed medication to make it through the day, and were unruly and disruptive. I was determined to work through my feelings, not be placed on medication, and leave the facility as soon as possible. I followed the rules and took guidance from the staff. Upon my discharge, to my surprise, my tenacious foster mom allowed me to return home.

Accept the Challenge: Tenaciously Activate the Opportunities and Gravitate to Relationships

Take advantage of every opportunity to bless others, especially our brothers and sisters in the family of faith. (Galatians 6:10) The righteous choose their friends carefully. (Proverbs 12:26)

During my hospital stay, there were tenacious individuals (gravitators) intentionally placed in my life to help me, like my home-based therapist. I had access to a host of different personal mental health fire extinguishers (gravitators) who helped me combat one-alarm, two-alarm, three- and four-alarm mental health fires. These extinguishers helped put out the fires of:

- the feeling of "no one gets me" by being understanding;
- fear of not being heard by giving me a chance to be heard;
- feeling that no one cares by showing me compassion;
- feeling invisible by smiling at me;
- being mistreated by treating me fairly;
- loneliness by making a connection with me;
- feeling I don't have potential by being nonjudgmental of me;
- feeling unloved by opening their hearts to me.

Accept the Challenge: Tenaciously Seek God First

But seek first the kingdom of God and his righteousness, and all these things will be added to you. (Matthew 6:33)

Recording artist Pharrell's song "Unspeakable Joy" references that level of pleasure that cannot be defined or connected to anything around you that makes you happy. The song tells the story of a person having a hard time and not being satisfied when they testify about the goodness of God. This person wants to be more precise, sharp, and on point about the blessings and goodness of God. While I have always believed in my God, I was that person in the song. Despite the years of adversity and attempts to numb the pain with education success and professional accomplishments, I had this nagging feeling that I was not living my life as God truly wanted me to live it. As a result, I felt incomplete and could not move forward without ensuring that I put God first in everything I did.

On November 20, 2022, I renewed my faith in God, got baptized, and was filled with the Holy Spirit. This experience focused me more on my God-given purpose, letting in what is needed to live out my purpose (establishing boundaries and seeking God first), and excusing myself (using time wisely and seeking God first). The desired change began to shine through.

Remember, our steps are ordered from the time we are conceived. Despite your age as you continue your life's journey, consider Accepting the Tenacity Challenge and Build Energy daily in tenacity.

1. BE tenacious by choosing to live life to the fullest by seeking a purpose-filled life.

2. BE more tenacious by opening up and letting in what you need emotionally, physically, financially, and physically to survive. Set boundaries for yourself and avoid allowing others to penetrate those boundaries.

3. BE more tenacious by acknowledging when you need to excuse yourself (#excuseme, working on me) from individuals and situations that hinder your progress in life. Seek the help you need and focus on a positive mindset.

4. BE more tenacious by pursuing and engaging in opportunities that will move your life forward. Gravitate toward tenacious individuals

connected to those opportunities and build relationships to support you on your purposeful journey.

5. BE more tenacious by first seeking spiritual guidance and allowing yourself to be driven by a higher power and purpose in life. Use that to embark on the Tenacity Challenge as you build your faith and conviction through your testimonies.

"No matter how heavy the challenges we face in our life, embrace optimism, perseverance, tenacity, and courage. Never lose faith and hope."
– Angelica Hopes, *Rhythm of a Heart, Music of a Soul*

Trisha Gordon accepted the challenge to inspire and empower others to discover their purpose and give their vision life through her speaking, writing, and signature visionary journal series. She employs techniques that identify one's purpose, establish boundaries, emphasize time management, promote activating opportunities, and aid in gravitating toward supportive individuals.

Trisha has a passion for empowering young girls and women and is a soon –to-be published author of *Accept the Challenge: Five Practical Techniques to Business Resilience and Strengthen Mental Wellbeing*, an interactive book with an accompanying journal, for middle and high school students.

Trisha is a nonprofit leader with more than thirty years of experience in the public and nonprofit sectors. She is a lifelong learner, holding degrees in Political Science/Pre-Law, Business Administration. and Human Resource Management, as well as a certificate in Entrepreneurship. She is a certified Malcolm Baldridge Quality Award Examiner and Women in Leadership ('61) alum.

Trisha currently serves as Vice President of Community Investment with United Way. She serves on a local RESPOND Advisory Committee with Foster and Adoptive Care Coalition, and on Girls in the Know's Board, and is a Big with Big Brothers Big Sisters of Eastern Missouri.

Trisha enjoys spending time with family and friends, indulging in fitness activities, creating literary works, writing, reading, and traveling.

Courtney Kuchar

Tenacious Medical Unicorn

My husband and I finished the kids' bedtime routine with prayers, and then Chuck and I were off for our evening time together. It was the middle of October, and the NBA playoffs were in full force. I finished my nightly routine, climbed into bed, and began scrolling social media on my phone while he watched the game intently. With the excitement of the game, my attention was pulled in multiple directions—TV to phone to TV—until my full attention went to the lump on my chest that my fingers had just discovered.

Although against all medical advice, my distracted scrolling quickly turned into attentive research. I searched "lump on breast" on Google, then "chances of breast cancer with no family history" until I finally decided to ask my husband about it. Not wanting to jump to conclusions, we both agreed that it did not feel normal and that we should see a doctor to clear our minds.

After many tests and biopsies, I was diagnosed with triple positive breast cancer. Me, a thirty-year-old wife and a mother to three young children, with no family history of breast cancer, began the fight for my life! Over the next twelve months, I endured chemotherapy, a double mastectomy, and reconstruction surgery. I was in a whirlwind, fighting for another day to watch my kids grow and make memories with my husband. While it seemed like those months were years, I was thrilled to finally ring that cancer-free bell on October 27, 2018!

During that year-long battle, there were many opportunities to show off my courageous personality. With zero knowledge or experience with cancer (praise God), my OBGYN recommended I go to the Women's Center and meet with the breast surgeon. The breast surgeon guided me through the "typical" process, and I chose her recommended oncologist and plastic surgeon. For a few weeks the treatment plan was "if this, then that."

A few more months and I was mastering the chemotherapy symptoms and rocking the bald head! Overwhelmed with information, tons and tons of support, meals, scans, tests, and appointments, I just wanted to follow the schedule. That was until my breast surgeon said she would be leaving the hospital and would not continue to oversee my care. She left the hospital just after my surgery in April 2018, before I had time for a follow-up. She transferred my care to a colleague, and my nurse coordinator did not change. I was midway through my fight and not about to let a little switch wear me down.

An oncology visit before chemotherapy revealed that the tumor was still present during surgery. Thankfully, this allowed for further pathology testing of the tumor, but it also required a revised treatment plan. My oncologist's treatment recommendations came with yet another blow: she, too, was leaving the hospital and needed to transfer my care to a colleague. This time, however, rather than following a typical schedule, it was time for me to get to work.

At the end of April 2018, aside from focusing on getting healthy, I was cancer-free and ready to really fight my battle. With everything else seemingly in place, I knew that my treatment should continue at Siteman Cancer Center in St. Louis, Missouri. All I needed to do was find the right doctor. After connecting with a few acquaintances, mostly from social media cancer groups, I transferred my treatment to a new oncologist.

For the next couple of years, my treatment plan was mostly seamless—an injection every month and a bone-strengthening infusion every six months. Every three months, I would have a routine checkup with my oncologist. She provided comfort and guidance. I always left feeling confident in my skin and healthier than when I arrived.

During a routine breast exam at the three-month checkup, my oncologist felt a concerning lump in my armpit. Being completely unaware of the lump until that moment, I was adamant about getting some diagnostic testing. My oncologist agreed, although she hesitated after learning that I'd recently received a pandemic virus vaccine. She decided to hold the diagnostic testing for four weeks unless the lump got noticeably larger. After asking for clarification of her decision, and pushing for more answers, she said she was not able to make a diagnostic testing appointment because it had been too close since receiving the vaccine. I left that appointment angry, confused, and defeated. But it was then that I knew I had to advocate for myself. God gave me that feeling, telling me to pursue testing because something was not right!

While I never expected this breast cancer journey, I know God has a plan for my life (Jeremiah 29:11). In the times of worry and concern, I was able to turn to prayer, and God showed me my path. With courage, control, and determination, it was proven that I must be my best advocate. I do not doubt that I was always receiving the best care, but with my health changing over time, my needs changed as well, which led to my care needing to change too.

I tried to schedule my own test but was unsuccessful. I reached out to my breast surgeon for a second opinion. Without seeing me first, my breast surgeon ordered an ultrasound, biopsy, and mammogram. Within seven days of my initial phone call to my breast surgeon, I was diagnosed with breast cancer, again!

This second diagnosis determined that I had recurrent triple positive breast cancer, isolated to a single lymph node in my left armpit. My fight continued with another change in my medical oncologist, this time by choice. With the help of my amazing support team, I requested a transfer of care to the medical oncologist at Siteman Cancer Center who has been researching HER2 positive breast cancer for more than thirty years.

Although I became a bit feisty to get my transfer request approved, I am happy to still be under that medical oncologist's care. He referred me to a great radiation oncologist who oversaw my seventeen treatments prior to another year of chemotherapy. His nurse coordinator has treated me like royalty, but, most importantly, I know that I am heard and valued. For example, when I experienced lower back pain, I was referred to a chiropractor, and when I had limited range of motion in my left arm, I was referred to a fabulous physical therapist.

With chemotherapy beginning in August 2021, I asked for the most aggressive path of treatment. My oncologist discovered during my first treatment that I had undiagnosed neutropenia, a low white blood cell disorder, which caused constant bacterial infections leading to hospitalizations and IV antibiotics. Not knowing if this was chemo-induced, chronic, or temporary, I began weekly blood tests to monitor my blood levels. When I found a pattern with low white blood cell counts and fatigue, I pressured my hematologist for an appointment with the head researcher of neutropenia at Siteman Cancer Center. With his proactiveness, I can maintain my counts with twice weekly at-home injections and regular lab work.

During an annual family trip to Gulf Shores, Alabama, in November 2021, I woke up with a swollen left breast and tight muscles in my arm. I knew something was wrong, so I went to a local ER and was diagnosed with an implant infection and presented with two choices—emergency surgery or return to my care team at home.

Feeling like I was in complete control, and eager to finish our week stay in Gulf Shores, my symptoms got progressively worse. After a twelve-hour drive home, I had a fever and increased pain, so off to the hospital I went, again. I was treated for an infection with IV antibiotics. A weekend stay in the hospital with no improvement sent me to my plastic surgeon from years prior, who informed me that my symptoms indicated an infected implant, most likely from radiation. He scheduled me for emergency surgery.

With absolute determination to beat my cancer, I held onto my strong faith and leaned into my family. As of June 2023, I am cancer-free for two years. Continued treatment and hormone therapy has kept the cancer at bay, but it wasn't just medicine that did the trick. I can lean into the medical team for education and research; however, it will forever be my courage, control, and self-advocacy that has and will keep me healthy! Persistence led me to be a two-time breast cancer survivor, and tenacity keeps me fighting daily.

Throughout this journey, I have tenaciously held on and chosen joy and faith. Much of the process has been a choice, and while fully advocating for myself, I followed the medical professionals for the treatment process, and mentally I chose joy every day. During moments of sadness, fear, and anxiety, I give myself twenty-four hours to feel that way, and on the advice of my best friend, Beth, go back to fighting for my life and choosing joy. I find joy in helping others, and while so many were there to help me and my family, I focused on how I could help others—patients, families, kids, friends—by sharing my story, inviting people over, and volunteering at the kids' school. My path through my cancer journey has not been as straightforward as I may have imagined it to be, but that is what life is all about—constantly getting back up and standing tall after being knocked down time and time again.

Courtney Kuchar is a two-time breast cancer survivor and a business-woman. She was born and raised in St. Louis, Missouri, and currently resides there with her supportive husband, Chuck, and three strong children, Charlie (11), Kennedy (9), and Sloane (7). Courtney graduated from Maryville University in St. Louis and graduated with a Sports Business Management degree. She actively cheers for her hometown St. Louis Cardinals and St. Louis Blues but is the biggest cheerleader for her kids. Courtney has been with Crown Packaging Corp. for more than ten years working in national accounts.

Karen S. Hoffman

Passing the Tenacity Torch

I want to start with the beginning of our nonprofit, Gateway to Dreams. "Beginnings" are not always obvious. It's when we look back in time that we realize "something" happened that started us on a new journey in life.

I was driving on the highway in St. Louis County when I emotionally broke down, crying and screaming at God. I wanted to know why I was not normal, why I could not just go and "get a job." I've always loved using my creativity to help others and solve problems. I felt like a misfit, and that God had made a huge mistake with me. A few miles later, I was apologizing to God. It wasn't his fault.

That evening, a local artist came to our home for a meeting. I had seen her adorable work at a local coffee shop, and we were going to brainstorm how we could use her art for a branding project. As she came in, she handed a book to me and said, "I haven't read this book, but I felt like I was supposed to give it to you." I understood that feeling. Many times, my intuition/God would whisper to take something to give to someone. The book was *The Dream Giver* by Bruce Wilkinson.

The book's message caught me totally off guard. The author wrote that everybody is born with a dream (or dreams) in them. Some people go for their dreams. Some do not. Some of us, say, meet a "Dream Champion." This caught my heart. They described the Dream Champion, and it was me. God sent me this book to help me understand that I was not a mistake, that he designed me deliberately. Wow. This feeling was a bit overwhelming, to know deeply that I was not a mistake.

Feeling more "on purpose," I dreamt of a future nonprofit called Gateway to Dreams. Here's the story of a close friend who was a Dream Champion for me.

In 2011, Suzi Tozer brought one of her dreams to me: to open a bookstore/café for local authors in a suburban St. Louis mall. Suzi was tenacious herself. She had been on a waiting list for a community space in the mall for a couple of years. In 2013, her space finally became available.

As we were working together on her dream, Suzi was diagnosed with deadly breast cancer. She had to decide whether to move forward with the bookstore or fight cancer. As a mom of three girls who had lost their father/her husband to an epileptic seizure a few years earlier, Suzi knew she had to be there for them. Suzi had to fight cancer. She set her dream aside.

Once Suzi made the decision to fight cancer and let her dream of creating a bookstore/café go, she had another idea. Suzi knew of my dream to one day start a nonprofit that would help people realize their dreams and goals. In May 2023, Suzi and I met at a local coffee shop, and she told me her decision to fight for her life. Then she mimed holding a large imaginary box in her hands and said she wanted to gift me her space in the mall—this very special space that she had waited so long for.

My immediate instinct was to say no. Suzi knew me very well, so before I could say it, she said, "Don't say no! Just think about it."

A few days later, I knew I had to tell her I was not going to do it. But then, on Thursday, May 30th, I woke up thinking about her gift and felt I was supposed to say yes. I know this might sound crazy, but I heard a voice saying, "Yes, it's Gateway to Dreams…Yes, it will be coaches and experts."

That day, my tenacity came on full strength when I said yes to Suzi, and to starting our nonprofit Gateway to Dreams.

Then the real dreaming began. What would Gateway to Dreams be? What could it be? What did it look like? How could I start this nonprofit with such a vague vision? How could I start a nonprofit without funding? Was I ready to do this? Yes, I was. I felt if I took the steps, God would be there. This proved to be true. But I knew I could not do it alone. With his help, we could do this.

I have always loved brainstorming (or DREAMstorming, as we say) to help others with their dreams and goals. I decided to start there. I asked business friends and associates to attend a brainstorming session. Chesterfield Mall's management was amazing while we worked out our vision for Gateway to Dreams. Over a two-week period, we held four different brainstorming/dream storming sessions in our future space, and during those meetings two ideas were put into effect immediately.

One idea was that we would have "members" who would pay a monthly membership fee to belong to Gateway to Dreams. We immediately received payments.

At another meeting, one attendee suggested that we needed to meet *every week* to work on the nonprofit and move us forward. Every week? Really? Who would make a commitment like that? I was shocked to see how many people believed in me and Gateway to Dreams and attended weekly.

Every week between July and October 2013, every week, so many people showed up for ninety-minute gatherings. We shared ideas, and the community began building our website and creating marketing materials, while others outside of this group helped with office furniture, decorating, and painting. It was so crazy, magical, and full of love and support!

We later named this group of amazing people our "Launch Ambassadors."

In October 2013 we hosted a silent auction, and, again, so many people donated things! Our team helped make all the auction items look gorgeous. One ambassador brought cases of new books; people donated gift certificates. During this time, a Launch Ambassador bought our soft seating furniture! She believed in GTD and assured me that the money would come to pay for all it. She was right; all items were paid for by the silent auction proceeds, with money left over.

Our official Grand Opening was in January 2014. In business as a 501(c)(3), we have always hosted monthly events, created to help people share their dreams, receive support, and grow personally and professionally.

Early on, a woman in her late seventies came in to share her dream. She was an internationally known animal photographer. She dreamed of traveling to France, where a bonobo ape she cared about had been moved. Financially, the trip was out of her reach. We invited this dreamer to share her dream. People gave her gifts ranging from $10 to $400, and she realized her dream, traveled to France, and took photos of her beloved bonobo. She was certainly tenacious as well!

Our 1,700 square foot space became our home, and in the fall of 2015, mall management asked us if we might be interested in a larger space. It was over 6,400 square feet for almost the same rent we were currently paying! This deal was too good to turn down. We remained focused on serving our members. We also stayed tenacious.

In 2018 and 2019 we added The Impact Awards program, to recognize individuals and small nonprofits who were making a difference in our community.

In 2020, as the pandemic closed our world down, our future was uncertain. The current model meant that members met face-to-face! Again, tenaciously, we kept going. Thanks to the virtual meeting platform Zoom, and an amazing member who taught us how to use it, we created a caring community online.

Eventually, our nonprofit was impacted financially. But again, tenaciously, we kept going. I think that trust and being tenacious go hand in hand. Finally, in June 2022 we reopened our doors. It was slow to rebuild our attendance, but we did it, together.

As the founder and executive director, I was exhausted. The stress of operating our nonprofit during the pandemic was hard. I also caught the virus in November 2020 and ended up with pneumonia, was in and out of the hospital, and months later was diagnosed with long-term side effects from the virus.

I had to decide: Could I keep going? It took me four days, but eventually I decided that I was done. This is where another miracle of tenacity showed up.

I shared where I was mentally and physically with Missy Coleman and Heidi Maxwell, the two volunteers who cochaired one of our most popular programs, Connecting & Promoting Women. The next day they both asked if they could join the board and take on more responsibilities to take things off my shoulders. They loved Gateway, and they wanted us to stay the course. They believed in our vision, our mission, and our community.

I had been tenacious for more than eight years, and I was exhausted. But Heidi and Missy were tenacious too. They wanted to pick up the torch and offered their support to give me space to breathe and recover.

The torch of tenacity was passed on.

Here's what I've learned about tenacity, from my friend Suzi all the way to Heidi and Missy:

1. If you have a dream, but not all the pieces are there, you can still proceed, tenaciously, without knowing how it will all work out. People and situations almost magically appear to help.

2. When we are being tenacious, things will and should evolve. The dream may change to something better and different than what we originally thought we wanted.

3. Being tenacious can wear us out. Sometimes "letting go" attracts others to be tenacious for us and carry on the dream.

Karen S. Hoffman is a speaker and coauthor of *The Art of Barter-How to Trade for Almost Anything* and *Building Your Business through Relationships: Contacts Connections Collaboration and Crisis.* Always an entrepreneur, she is a cocreator of several programs: The Joy of Goals, Your Collaborative Board, Connecting & Promoting Women, Write Your Book Right Now, NonProfits Rock St. Louis, and the magazine *Be the Change–St. Louis,* and more. Karen's awards and recognitions include: the former Regional Commerce & Growth Association "Pacesetter Award" for helping Small Businesses; The Small Business Administration Award for helping Home Based Businesses; *The Small Business Monthly's 100 People to Know in St. Louis;* eWomen Network International Business Matchmaker of the Year; as well as other recognition.

Karen hopes that Gateway to Dreams continues to impact women entrepreneurs and small nonprofits. Her motto: ***"When you KNOW your dreams, and you SHARE your dreams, people can help you REACH your dreams."***

Helen Jardine

Spell It Out

"He's gone," my brother said when I met him at the hospital. "Dad's gone." I was shocked to hear those words *Wait! What?* He was just going to the hospital because he was dehydrated and nauseated from the chemotherapy. They said at least twelve to eighteen months, not six weeks. How was this possible? So many thoughts were spinning in my head. So many decisions to handle. So many details to arrange. We had handled them together—Dad, my brothers, and me—when my mom passed away four years earlier.

My mom had been sick for quite a while before she passed. I had just had lunch with my dad a few weeks before for his seventy-seventh birthday. He was strong, vibrant, full of life. The diagnosis that he had an aggressive form of leukemia was hard to believe. *There must be some mistake*, I'd thought.

There was not.

I remember standing in the receiving line at the church, numbly greeting friends and family as they shared stories and were in equal disbelief. I was thinking, "Wow, now I'm an orphan." An odd thought to have in my fifties, until another adult who'd lost both his parents said, "Well, we have something in common. We're both orphans."

As I sat in the pew trying to hold it together without much success, I held hands with Sue, a wonderful woman my dad had met and married after my mom passed away. Listening to each of my brothers give a eulogy was tough and comforting. My youngest brother chose to remember my dad in a way that my dad was known for. My dad enjoyed sharing his thoughts or reflecting on a topic by taking a word or idea and using the letters from the word to prompt thoughts about it. So I listened as my brother used each letter from my dad's first and last name to share a memory about him. And when he got to the final letter of the last name, which is a "D," my brother simply said, "Dad."

As the years have passed, there have been multiple times I've wished I could still physically talk with my parents, especially as new challenges in life come up. I often wonder, "What would they think or suggest?" In these times, I remember through their examples and encouragement that my parents instilled in me not only the courage and belief in myself to push through when facing obstacles but the tenacity to persist in the face of hardships and difficulties.

Growing up, both my parents were supportive and encouraging (thankfully) even in the face of some of our crazy ideas and life's unexpected curveballs. One big example of this is when I leapt with both feet into being an entrepreneur at age twenty-four. I'd been downsized at the nonprofit organization I was working for when they lost funding for their video production department. Once the dust settled, there were four of us under the age of thirty who started our own bilingual Spanish/English video production company.

Since the department was closing, we had a couple of the previous clients to call on. Our previous employer allowed us to temporarily work out of their basement to get our feet underneath us. Thankfully, my parents let me move back in with them. They also believed in the dream enough to lend us start-up funds, which we paid back early. I explored every free business resource through the Small Business Administration and Service

Corps of Retired Executives and took women entrepreneur classes at the local community college to help land the company a $100,000 bank loan to purchase equipment. Failing wasn't an option. Pushing through, finding a way, and overcoming obstacles was the only focus.

A few months into the venture, one of our supporters at the previous company passed away, and a board member confronted me, saying, "Look, we never thought you would be successful; that's why we let you stay." The writing on the wall was clear, so we moved into five hundred square feet of office space consisting of three rooms. One became an edit suite. Another, an equipment room/office for one of the partners. The other three of us crowded our desks, mini fridge with microwave on top, and a couple of chairs into the largest room for a makeshift workspace, kitchen/lobby combo. We were determined to make this work.

As anyone who has ever started their own business knows, success is not a straight line. Over the fourteen years of that company, we celebrated some amazing highs, such as winning awards and being featured in *Fortune Small Business Magazine*, and some incredible lows, like sometimes wondering how we were going to make payroll.

Throughout the years, my parents would come to our business anniversary events, recommend us to people they thought could use our services, and be a listening ear or shoulder to cry on.

My business partners and I were single when we started the company, and as our lives changed with many of us marrying and having children, we eventually decided to go our separate ways. But the lessons of those years taught me tenacity in working toward my goals and following my dreams.

In 2008, in the middle of a recession, I transitioned into a brand-new career field with some entrepreneurial battle scars. I was able to put my knowledge of running a business to use in new ways by coaching financial advisors on how to think like business owners.

Over the years, as my dad and I would meet for our monthly father/daughter lunches, we would periodically reflect on life, my entrepreneurial journey, our real estate investment and stock market adventures, and my current career, which has had a few iterations.

Often, we would remind each other of one of our favorite quotes by T.S. Eliot: "Only those who will risk going too far can possibly find out how far one can go."

There are many times when I miss both my parents and still think, "Wow, I know they'd know what to do in this situation. I wish they were here."

As I was reflecting on tenacity for this chapter, I remembered my father's funeral and how my brother used how my dad liked to spell words out and reflect on them to help my brother gain insight and healing, which he so eloquently shared with the attendees. So, as I thought about how helpful this exercise had been for my brother and my dad, I decided I would try it and see what came to me. And so, the words began to flow onto the page.

This too shall pass. Take the challenges one day at a time. The answers will come. You don't have to solve it all at once, and this time of struggle will not last forever.

Everything is always working out for you. Trust. Know. Connect with All That Is—God-Source. You have what you need, or the people, places, solutions will be provided for you. You are not alone. Detours can be redirections on your path.

Never give up...hope, belief, knowing you are loved. New information may provide ideas, new directions, strategies. Things may not work out exactly as you had planned. Be flexible. A "no" will not kill you, and you are stronger, more resourceful, and more capable than you think you are! This is a "dig deep" experience, allowing you to discover gifts you didn't know you had.

All is in Divine Timing. People, resources, and opportunities are aligning for you and your success. This is an opportunity to practice patience.

Completely worthy. Yes, you are. This situation and circumstance does not define you or your value. You are worthy simply because you exist.

I am enough. There is nothing you need to do, be, have, or become. You are enough. You are a powerful creator. Step into all that you are and empower yourself. What I seek, seeks me.

Totally deserve success. Why not you? You are just as deserving as anyone else. Do not doubt that success can be yours.

You can do it! You are capable and competent. You can achieve your goals and dreams!

Dear Readers, I encourage you to try this exercise of spelling out words or phrases and seeing what new insights and ideas come to you.

Writing this chapter and reflecting on the theme of tenacity has given me a great reminder that my dad and mom are still here with me in the whispers of my soul. When I face challenges, I hear him reminding me:

This too shall pass.

Everything is always working out for you.

Never give up…hope, belief, knowing you are loved.

All is in Divine Timing.

Completely worthy.

I *am* enough.

Totally deserve success.

You can do it!

-Dad

Helen Jardine, CLU˚, ChFC˚, CFP˚, CASL˚, RICP˚, CLF˚ is the first female district director with Northwestern Mutual in St. Louis. In addition to helping clients put plans in place to achieve their financial goals and dreams, she has the privilege of selecting and training talented people who are seeking a career with impact and want to make our communities *the* most financially secure in the world. She loves coaching people to help them develop and achieve their potential. She is certified in the Foundations of Women-Centered Coaching.

Prior to joining Northwestern Mutual, she was a co-owner of Cor Productions, Inc., a bilingual video production and marketing company located in St. Louis, Missouri. She has also founded and run two women's networking and mastermind groups.

Outside the office, she enjoys spending time with her family and friends. She and her husband, Bill, have been married since 1997. They have two children, Danielle and Tyler..

Destini Flemons

Testimony to Tenacity

I welcome this opportunity to share my story and hope that it motivates and even inspires others to persevere through life's hurdles. My chapter gives a quick look into how I overcame the curveballs that came my way in life to become the person I am today.

I grew up in St. Louis with my mom, dad, younger sister, and grandma. I felt fairly secure and stable through all those years. In 2017, I entered McCluer North High School in Florissant, Missouri. That is when everything changed. The stability and life that I had no longer existed, and overnight I went from a child sheltered from life's problems to a young adult struggling to adapt to a new reality.

Not only was I experiencing the issues common to starting as a freshman in a new school, but then my parents split up. This new living situation required my mother to work long hours to provide for my sister and me. The change also put a lot on me. I was upset and confused by their breakup, and I became a second mother (with cooking, homework, etc.) to my younger sibling.

Not long after that, my nana (my grandma on my mother's side) experienced a worsening heart condition. She required more support from the family, and we were all worried about her condition. Following months of treatments and assessments, she was put on a list for a heart transplant.

After many weeks of prayers and doctor visits, she was blessed with a successful heart transplant. It was an amazing and thankful moment in our house! But then she needed many more weeks of support from the family during her physical therapy. I am happy to say that she has fully recovered and is now living the full life she once lived. Through all this, I continued in school but was barely holding it all together, feeling overwhelmed by helping with the house, my sister, my mom, and my nana.

Then I lost one of my closest friends. She was killed by a drunk driver. I was in shock. We were both just fourteen years old. I could not believe this was all happening.

Despite all that I was dealing with in my life, I set a goal to learn more about technology. To do that, I wanted to enroll in my school's partner program with North County Technical High School.

To get accepted to the program, I needed to keep my grades up. Freshman and sophomore years were very hard, but I took one week at a time and kept on top of each class and got my homework in on time. I even started taking an IT course, and by the end of my sophomore year I had earned the Microsoft Technology Associate (MTA) certification. That course provides fundamental technological knowledge, and I discovered that I really like Information Technology (IT). This class started my interest in an IT career. I found my love for coding in that class.

Life threw me another curveball in my junior year in high school, one of the most important years in high school, in my opinion. The year was 2020, and the country was shut down due to the pandemic. I was forced to hold down things on the home front and adapt to a brand-new style of learning as well. My whole family was trying to figure out how to adapt to this new world. Then we were hit with a big loss that affected my mom's job, my sister's schooling, even my nana's lifestyle. It felt like I was back at square one. I knew, though, that I had to keep going. I kept trying to learn online through my junior and senior year. It was not easy.

That is about the time in my senior year that I heard about a new program called Access Point. It was the first IT program I had ever seen at a school like mine. Access Point was different because it promised a full-time job when the program was completed. Something like this had never been heard of in my school district. I realized that this program could have a huge impact on my life. What a blessing it would be to be able to help my mom out at my young age! Seeing where I am today and where I was then brings tears to my eyes as I write this.

I was nervous to apply, but I submitted my application after a few conversations with my family. After a few interviews, I was in! I was so proud of myself as I was stepping up to this new chapter called adulthood. But it wasn't an easy program. I faced many challenges. I was having to balance my regular senior year, plus the Access Point training, and helping at home. Two of the Access Point leaders, Jason and Christy, provided a lot of support during the course and have continued to provide support even after I got my job. Without their encouraging conversations, I probably would have given up on the program. I graduated from high school in May of 2021, completed more training through the summer, and then six more months of apprenticeship at the Access Employer partner, Evernorth. In March of 2022 I completed the apprenticeship, and, as promised, Evernorth hired me for a full-time position, with benefits, as an application developer analyst.

During this time, my mom experienced some very serious health challenges, which meant I needed to provide more support for my younger sister. Not only did I have the financial means to help at home, but my managers were understanding and willing to provide some creative workarounds so that I could meet expectations at work and at home. I am so appreciative of what this company has done to give me this stability and an IT career.

So, what is next? I just bought my dream car and started saving for my dream house!

What is my message for you? Take it from me—just because there are bumps in the road doesn't mean that you should give up. I am very grateful that I had support from my family to hold my head high and keep persevering. Without my family and God, I probably wouldn't have been in a place where I could take advantage of a program like Access Point. I put in a lot of hard work to achieve this dream. But I've learned that, if you keep at it, there will likely be a rainbow at the end of the storm.

So here I am. My cybersecurity degree is almost complete, and I am working full-time pursuing my IT career in that field. I found the opportunity and the confidence to go after a job like this because of programs like *Access Point and companies like Evernorth, who took a chance and believed in me, even through all the ups and downs.*

Destini Flemons is an Application Development Associate Analyst at Ever-north, where she is also part of the Diversity Investment Venture (DIVE) career development initiative. She is currently completing her associate degree in Cyber Security at St. Louis Community College. Destini graduated in 2021 from McCluer North High School in St. Louis, Missouri, and was part of the inaugural class of the Access Point Program (www. AccessPointProgram.com). She has served as a presenter to students and educators, talking about her Access Point journey and her entry into the Information Technology field. Destini exemplifies what tenacity is about through her drive to overcome barriers and challenges in her life that would have proven insurmountable to many..

Jaiah Conners

Opportunity + Talent + Tenacity = Success

"The most disrespected person in America is the black woman.
The most unprotected person in America is the black woman.
The most neglected person in America is the black woman."

- Malcolm X

I remember hearing the poem "Lost Voices" read by the authors Darius Simpson and Scout Bostley. "The first day I realized I was black," Darius said, when his microphone cut out. Scout finished his speech for him because her mic remained live. Darius looked at her in confusion as he mouthed the words along with her. Scout said, "As a woman," when suddenly the microphone switched to Darius and he finished the speech. She grabs at her throat, mouthing the words into her silent mic.

My voice has often been silenced, as a Black woman, when others speak over me and my struggles. I understand both Darius's and Scout's experiences, but I'm unable to live my life solely as a Black person or a woman. I am a dark-skinned, monoracial Black woman.

In school, my skin tone, my body, and my overall appearance was mocked by others. Teachers would ignore them, as if I hadn't been intentionally humiliated. When those same kids would falsely accuse me of something, I wasn't asked for my perspective but immediately threatened with suspension. I looked into any mirror and thought, "You'd be prettier if you were lighter." In a life of hearing "You aren't good enough," you start to believe it.

I struggled with "fitting in." I struggled in writing this piece, debating whether or not to add vital, below-the-surface attributes of myself. I am a Black pomosexual Christian woman. I hate the concept of "coming out," so I didn't; I just started existing freely. It's hard to do when you're surrounded by people who are simply anti-you. Though I grew up as a Christian, I no longer subscribe to church dogma. I prefer to demonstrate firmness of faith without the rules and expectations placed on me. The basis of Christianity is to spread love and kindness. A coterie of people telling me who I'm "allowed" to spread this love to isn't kin to me. Living this way has made my relationship with God flourish in ways it hadn't before.

Growing up, I felt that I was supposed to be against anything "not normal," and I hurt many people in the process. This behavior was very damaging considering the fact that I'm not "normal." And this goes way beyond my sexuality. Seeing different as a bad thing while simultaneously being different affected how I do things now. I am still afraid to fully express myself because I feel judged, though I used to be the faultfinder. Then I realized that they don't build statues or create artwork to honor critics.

Art is a gift I was put here to do and is how people will remember me when I'm gone. "Paper" was my nickname growing up because wherever I went, that was the first thing I'd ask for to draw on. To the dreaded question, "What do you want to be when you grow up?" I answered, "An artist." My first job, at fourteen, was with St. Louis ArtWorks. I created in a variety of art forms including printmaking, sculpting, and graphic design. I look back on those days fondly as a time when I got paid for the hobbies I love.

Art is the creation of something beautiful. My artistry doesn't have to stop at traditional drawing or painting. My writing ability has come to overshadow my painting, my eye for fashion, traditional art, etc.

In 2021, my aunt urged my mom to get me into software coding classes. There is a visible lack of Black female coders, and I loved the idea of representing an underrepresented community. My senior year at University City High, I enrolled in a LaunchCode class. Most of the students were boys, but it didn't bother me. There were three other Black girls, but they soon dropped the class. There were classmates who had been coding for years, or who caught on faster than I did, but my teacher always encouraged me. I greatly appreciated it. One day after class he reminded me of the need to get more Black women into the field. Then, our Dean of Students introduced me to the program Access Point. With Access Point, an apprenticeship was guaranteed after studying. It felt forward-thinking. In an interview with the dean and my future professor, I was asked a question that I'd soon hear a lot: "What do you work for, what drives you, motivates you?"

I started Access Point my senior year while working two part-time jobs. After high school, I spent my summer studying Java and JavaScript. I was nervous meeting other students in person, but there aren't words to explain how welcoming everyone was. It usually takes a long time for me to open up even a little, but it felt like a safe space. I genuinely appreciate all of their friendships.

We were introduced to people from the companies who would hire us. I was accepted by my first choice, Mastercard. Then things felt more *serious*. We approached our classes like a job. Every class started with a stand-up meeting, working in teams at the Daugherty office. At graduation, we presented our capstone projects. A great memory of mine was watching my peers show off everything we worked on—our growth, technically, but also as people. I was so proud of all of us. We said we would do it and we did!

In the program, I learned resilience, to not let difficulties take me down, and to make time for the things I cared about. My professors taught me patience and how to positively grasp the attention of others. They supported me in ways that I needed to succeed.

My mentors helped me find my way around the business world and improve my tech skills.

My tech mentor has become a friend. As the oldest daughter in my family, it's nice to see her as an older-sister archetype. She gives things to me straight and comforts me when I get impostor syndrome. It's easy to talk with her about the life I want to create and the things I'm passionate about. She is someone I'd like to be like in my future.

My first time on the Mastercard campus, I felt like I was in a movie scene. Working at a campus that big with so much security was bizarre, but the views from the windows were gorgeous.

In a meeting on my first day, I put my head down often, so I didn't get distracted by things happening around me. I have issues with attention sometimes. But putting your head down at work looks like you're sleeping. I made a terrible first impression, but in my opinion, this set me up to show that much more growth!

Later on, I started to feel intimidated by my team leader, not because of anything he said or did but because he was someone I wanted to impress. I felt below everyone else because I had far less experience. I was afraid I'd let everyone down: my family, the Access Point team, my peers, my team at Mastercard, even myself. I wanted to say the right things, speak to the right people, and make the right decisions. I felt I'd end up doing it all wrong.

My team at Mastercard has shown nothing but kindness and support. My mentors have been there for me when I needed help. Occasionally

I thought I was burdening people because I needed things explained to me in depth. There have been times when the team had more faith in my skills than I did. I thought I should be smarter or that I should catch on as quickly as everyone else. I'm still trying to overcome this mindset. At the end of the day, though, I'm able to say I did my best. My best was often good enough. Overthinking is still an issue for me, but I put things more into perspective after I heard this lighthearted quote from Bob The Drag Queen: "If you're a perfectionist, you're never going to go onstage until you're perfect. You're never going to be perfect, so just hit the stage."

That interview question has popped up often: "What do you work for, what drives you, motivates you?" The answer is: my art. With my career, I can afford to fund my hobbies in music, painting, digital art, and fashion—all the things I love. I may write and illustrate a few children's books. I love the beautiful scenery around the world, and I can finally travel! I'm considering getting a couple of pets, and I'd love to be a home-owner in my twenties.

I want to show the Access Point team that supporting me wasn't a mistake. I want the Mastercard team to see my growth. I want everyone who negatively affected me in any way to see that their critiques didn't affect the path intended for me. I want to be able to help support my family. I want to be proof to little girls who look in the mirror and wish that they were anybody else (like I did) that it does get better—so much better.

It's almost been a year since starting at Mastercard. I'm planning to take more college classes. I've been graced to live through so many opportunities I never could have seen myself doing at eighteen. This is just the beginning of my story, and if I'm able to do this much in nineteen years, I'm ecstatic to see what else is in store for me. I know that I have so many people in my corner cheering me on, waiting to see what I do with everything that I worked for. To them, I will be forever grateful.

Jaiah Conners is a software engineer at Mastercard, a 2022 graduate of University City High School in St. Louis, Missouri and the Access Point Program. She is an avid artist and devoted to her family. Jaiah is continuing her education in pursuit of a bachelor's degree. She is at the beginning of what will surely be a highly successful career in Information Technology and is a proud ambassador for Access Point (www.AccessPointProgram.com) and her community. Jaiah is proving through personal example that opportunity, combined with dedication, talent, and tenacity, leads to success.

Dr. Adrienne Fox-Ray

The Power of Re-

I don't ever remember being called tenacious. Being tenacious was subtly encouraged but not nurtured in my earlier years. Respect, responsibility, kindness, and caring were emphasized in school and at home. My parents may not have encouraged the tenacious spirit, but tenaciousness was evident in my household. For instance, in our bathroom, my dad posted a quote on the door so you'd read it each time you closed it. The quote: "It doesn't matter whether you're the lion or a gazelle; when the sun comes up, you'd better be running." Although I understood the quote, I was not prepared to experience how this quote and other similar things would appear in my life. In reflection, it ties closely to something else my dad would say: "Adrienne, you will always have to work harder than your counterpart." Both these quotes shaped my viewpoint of the world.

At a young age, I realized that competition and challenges existed and were a natural part of becoming an adult. Even with advice from family members, friends, and colleagues, I could not be saved from making some huge mistakes. Although I learned to be fearlessly tenacious, I now wish a mentor, friend, or family member would have shared the following with me. First, remain faithful because failure is a part of everyone's journey. That's how we learn. My second piece of advice would be to embrace the power of the prefix "Re-" because it means "again." Finally, own your

power and be yourself, because no one else is like you. In this chapter, I intend to share the journey that helped me realize the importance of being faithful, embracing the power of the prefix "Re-," and owning your power.

In the Bible, the Book of Jeremiah (29:11) states: "'For I know the plans I have for you,' declares the Lord, 'plans to prosper you and not to harm you, plans to give you hope and a future.'" Even if you are not religious, this quote can still be applicable. I wholeheartedly believe that each person's pathway will be filled with plans for greatness. Although obstacles, challenges, and heartache may divert those paths, the ultimate goal is to be fruitful and prosperous. I must admit that I am not a "live in the present" person. I have always felt I was ten seconds behind everyone else. I daydream and constantly get caught in my thoughts. In high school, my friends would always ask, "Adrienne, are you there?" because I would stare off into the distance and tune everything out. Others would need to snap me out of my trance. Essentially, something significant would need to happen for me to react. In 2007, that's what happened.

I was twenty-one weeks pregnant with my oldest son, Tyree, and my water broke. My husband and I rushed to the hospital and were told by our doctor that he was not viable until twenty-four weeks, and if I developed an infection we would have to deliver him early. Unfortunately, that happened, and he did not survive. At twenty-three years of age, I experienced a tremendous loss. Death was one of the first obstacles to my prosperity, and it was one of the first moments I can remember when I questioned my faith and purpose of life. Shortly after that, I got pregnant again. I was terrified that I would experience the same fate. That's what fear does to you—it makes you feel like you are in a trance until something snaps you out. For me, the daydreaming ended when I had finally passed twenty-one weeks. I knew that we were going to deliver a healthy baby boy. As I felt the veil of fear lifting, my faith was tested again. At twenty-two weeks, my water broke again, and my husband and I were given the same prognosis. This baby was not viable and would not survive if I delivered him before twenty-four weeks' gestation. I distinctly remember feeling fear encroaching on my spirit.

Something needed to snap me out of it, and that's just what happened: God spoke to me. He said, "Fight!" His plan for my future was not that I would be heartbroken once again. Because of my earlier loss, I could better advocate for my son's survival. I refused bedrest at home, requested sonograms to determine amniotic fluid level, and, finally, we changed OBGYN doctors. I didn't know this then, but this was the best decision, because this doctor knew what we had experienced earlier and vowed to do whatever was needed. My son is now fourteen years old, and although he has some challenges, he is strong and healthy. That's the thing about tenacity: you must trust the process even if you cannot see the end. You must believe and have faith that the plans this world has for you are to prosper you. Even amid challenging times, it prepares you for the future.

Did you know that the prefix "re-" means "again," "back," or it indicates repetition? That's powerful! It is freeing to know there is always a chance to try something repeatedly until you are satisfied. This only applies if you are aware of it. Just like with the birth of my son Timothy, when I had the opportunity to reshape my family's future. Sometimes I feel like I am on a hamster wheel, running the same path each day, and occasionally, if I am cognizant, I realize I am experiencing the same thing again. Refocus, reenergize, reshape, and reignite was the theme of my career for three years while I completed my doctoral studies.

Similarly, the power of "re-" allowed me to focus mentally on my research to glean helpful tips and recommendations for future research. The power of "re-" allowed me to be energized after a stressful year of pandemic mandates. The systems of inequity within the education system were highlighted, and educators continue to transition to other careers for various reasons. Being able to find the motivation to commit to another year took energy. The power of "re-" allowed me to shape a career path in education. Finally, it has ignited my passion for supporting teachers while they support students in attaining their goals. Rethink, refocus, reshape, reignite, and empower one's ability to start again! Tenacity is the ability to continue and power through repeatedly until goals are achieved.

Michelle Obama stated, "There's power in allowing yourself to be known and heard, owning your unique story, and using your authentic voice. And there's grace in being willing to know and hear others. We need to do a better job of putting ourselves higher on our own to-do list." Learning to show up in every space as your authentic self is part of being tenacious. Authenticity is like body armor; it's the first level of protection when you need to persist. When you must stay engaged, stick to it and remain determined. Authenticity is protection because it encourages empathy and it encourages connections. The more authentic you are, the more likely you are to build strong relationships with others.

Last year, I decided to apply for several leadership roles. In addition to completing graduate courses and professional and personal responsibilities, I interviewed for competitive leadership positions in neighboring school districts. Well, it didn't turn out the way I hoped. I was devastated when I didn't move past the screening process at my building. The younger Adrienne would have returned to work and pretended I wasn't emotionally affected, even though the authentic Adrienne knew she needed time. I am happy to report that I took a few days off. I gathered myself and planned to avoid any unnecessary stress. I set boundaries, and I permitted myself not to engage. I no longer pretend to be happy with decisions when I'm not, and I engage when I want to because that's who I am. Tenacity requires mental strength, and I've learned that the only way to strengthen my inner being is by being me 100 percent of the time.

If you asked me to describe myself, I wouldn't describe myself as tenacious. Tenacity is an underlying trait that needs to be subtly strengthened. Tenacity is woven through each obstacle a person persists through; it's repeatedly in process and reinforces authenticity. Now, looking back, I see how my family took me down this tenacious path, and I'm all the better for it!

Dr. Adrienne Fox-Ray is an award-winning educator, mother, wife, and passionate leader. She began her career in education in 2006 in the St. Louis area as a fourth-grade teacher. Her love of education has led her to earning a master's in Educational Technology and Reading from Webster University and a master's in Administration and Doctorate in Teacher Leadership from Maryville University. Through her varied experiences as an educator, she believes that all students deserve unlimited opportunities and access to various experiences. All children are filled with great potential; it is the educator's privilege to witness the journey. In her free time, she enjoys spending time with family and friends, listening to books, and binge-watching TV series..

Tracey Feldhake

There Is No One Like You

When I was invited to participate in this collaborative anthology, my initial, uncensored thought was, "Do they know me? Do they know that I am nothing special? Do they know I have nothing to offer the world?" I was humbled and honored, but I also felt equally terrified and undeserving. I knew if I said yes, my chapter and my story would be bound next to chapters and stories from incredibly successful businesswomen, powerful community leaders, and inspiring entrepreneurs. It made me wonder, "Who am I compared to these other women whose stories will likely be filled with tremendous successes?"

And then I caught myself—maybe this is exactly what I can offer in my chapter. Maybe the very thing I have been fighting internally for years will resonate with and matter to others as well. Maybe, just maybe, the very message—that none of us should ever allow ourselves to be defined by what we are not—is exactly what I need to share. Both for myself, as a documented reminder, and for the readers.

So here we are. As you read, I hope you realize that, like me, your story does not have to be exceptional. You already *are* exceptional. And your story is always worth sharing.

For each of us, our life story is an amalgamation of chapters of evolution and revolution. The happy and sad, the ups and downs, the twists and turns of everyday life—we all experience them, regardless of our character, title, purpose, or role. I am sure this is a topic we have each given a great deal of thought. But just for a minute, let's imagine we could fly up and sit among the stars in the sky. If we could view ourselves from another perspective, zoom out from our day-to-day to see the world around us, what would we see?

Over the course of our lives, there have undoubtedly been and will assuredly continue to be several pivotal moments, small or large, where the subsequent decision and that next first step will change your lives forever. Would we have made the same decisions we made in the past? Would it change which decisions we would make in the future?

When I was a little girl, I watched the film production of the 1900 children's novel *The Wonderful Wizard of Oz* by author L. Frank Baum over and over again, first, until I knew all the words, and then until I quite literally wore out the magnetic tape of the VHS. For those unfamiliar, Dorothy is a tenacious young farm girl from Kansas who struggles with isolation and purposelessness in a proverbial black-and-white world. In the midst of a tragedy, she dreams of an adventure in a fictional world bursting with color and exceptional characters. Dorothy and her new friends are faced with an inconceivable task complicated by their individual self-perceived weaknesses.

The enduring theme of the story, "if I only had a brain, a heart, the nerve, a home," has always resonated and stuck with me. The Scarecrow embodies the quest for sound theory and solid understanding. The Tinman searches for the authentic sharing and giving of love. The Cowardly Lion strives for valiant courage and strength of self. Dorothy desperately seeks a sense of belonging and self-assurance.

We can each take this story theme and apply it to our individual lives. Is it enough for us to just have these desires, these dreams for our future?

These "if I only's" set a basis for our personal journey, but it is what we chose to do with our dreams, if we choose to fight for ourselves, that will ultimately define who we are. That fight is our power. That fight makes us everything this world needs.

The story never tells you what happens after the "if I only" dreams of the beloved characters are realized. Perhaps the ending is left to our imaginations because that is what living is all about, realizing these values and fighting for our dreams in ourselves—just like the Scarecrow, the Tinman, the Cowardly Lion, and Dorothy did—then writing the next chapters of our own story.

I believe Dorothy and her friends each learned that they already embodied exactly what they sought in the world. I believe they fought to not only understand and embrace that, but they took that next step and fought for the intellectual awareness, emotional understanding, and self-confidence to share their respective perceived weaknesses as powerful and dynamic strengths with their family, friends, and communities. They individually and collectively accomplished what seemed impossible.

The story of *The Wonderful Wizard of Oz* shows us that we do not have to go far, we do not have to go "somewhere over the rainbow" and back to find our inner strengths for these fights, to achieve our dreams, and to matter to the world. We can do that right here, starting right now, in our own backyard.

I have written many chapters in my personal story, and whether good or bad, inspiring or insightful, dramatic or tragic, they all still reflect this theme. Through immense personal loss, trauma, grief, overwhelming fear, failed relationships, adoptions, new starts, incredible opportunities, and unconditional love, I have lived, survived, and even thrived through the worst and the best. And, like Dorothy, the one thing I have steadfastly relied upon is my tenacity, the relentless spark within me that never stops burning but sometimes needs a little kindling and fuel.

Some days I had to be like the Scarecrow and draw on my resourcefulness and intelligence, even when I doubted if I had wisdom at all. Some days I felt like the Tinman, empty and cold, and yet I had to summon the inner strength to create and express the very empathy and love for which I longed. More than I like to admit, I found myself struggling like the Cowardly Lion to even believe in myself, let alone stay true to who I was in the face of many incredibly daunting situations and a perpetual self-defeating vortex of emotions. The Dorothy in me has yearned for "home" so deeply it felt like that need might shatter my heart. Yet I remained willing to face the unknown to find answers to the problems life tossed my way.

While I still may not lead in business or shine in the community or be the best example of, well, anything, I have always shown up for myself. Like the Scarecrow, Tinman, Cowardly Lion, and Dorothy, I have used my weaknesses as fuel for the fire to meld my strengths and generate a blazing brightness. I have fought for myself so that I could also fight for others, and I have never stopped fighting until I have won.

There is no place like home. There is no one like you. We can each practice and perfect our tenacity right where we are, mentally and emotionally as well as physically. Know and believe what you want, what you are capable of, what you deserve. Throw the full weight of your faith and the law of attraction behind it, and then launch yourself into the world and tackle it. Despite the obstacles and challenges, your reach will travel as far as you believe it can go. You will change the world.

You do not have to ever accept the darkness of the world around you as it is. You have the unwavering power and the potential to fully realize your knowledge, compassion, and strength to be a force for change to create the beautiful and color-filled world that you know is possible.

I wish I had something more profound to offer, something worthy of the enormity of the value and purpose of all that you are. But I leave you with this: Never think you do not have an impact. You have the worth and potential to change the world. Since the day you were created, you have already had everything you need within yourself.

Fight for that.

Fight for you.

Tracey Feldhake is a holistic systems engineer with several years of dynamic leadership experience, specifically within the defense and emergency response industries. She has been sought out to lead challenging teams and improve team dynamics and performance. Although she is an engineer by education, she is a problem solver by experience. She is dedicated to continuous growth, personally and professionally, and is committed to family, community, and country.

Tracey has encountered and embraced challenge and sacrifice on a personal level as well as professional, which has strengthened her resilient nature, flexibility to adapt to constantly changing circumstances, and ability to overcome adversity with a positive focus on the hidden opportunities.

Outside of work, Tracey also strives to affect a positive change in her community. She is a foster parent, a Safe Families Host Family and member of the Leadership Council, a homeschool mom, and an advocate for empowering others.

Ashley Nelson

HR EXECUTIVE

BARRIER BREAKER • MOTHER • ENTREPRENEUR

BOARD MEMBER • AUTHOR

Fuel Your Passion

www.linkedin.com/in/ashley-nelson-phr

Made in the USA
Monee, IL
10 May 2024

58296310R00164